OUR VERY OWN 2

Stories Celebrating
Adoptive Families

PARTRIDGE
A Penguin Random House Company

Edited by:
Annabel Middleton, abelle.middleton@gmail.com
Cover Photo by:
Gabriel Aiden Ng, hello@aidenvisuals.co

All proceeds less costs, if any, from the sale of this book will be channeled back to the work of TOUCH Adoption Services.

Print information available on the last page.

To order additional copies of this book, contact
Toll Free 800 101 2657 (Singapore)
Toll Free 1 800 81 7340 (Malaysia)
orders.singapore@partridgepublishing.com

www.partridgepublishing.com/singapore

stories are thought-provoking and insightful, showing that although adoptive parenting can be challenging, it can also bring tremendous joy with proper planning, support and understanding of children's development.

This is a wonderful resource book for both prospective and adoptive parents. It offers a comprehensive view through narratives on children's post-adoption adjustment, older child adoption and experience of adopting older children.

It was particularly interesting to read an adoptee's account validating the importance of a supportive family environment in helping adopted children achieve an integrated sense of identity, while "Part 2 – Sequels" gives an update on contributors who had shared their stories in the first book (published in 2010) and still continue to journey with their children as they grow.

Many families are also thankful to TOUCH Adoption Services for their continued support. Without the help of supportive professionals, the adoptive parenting journey would have been far more difficult.

These stories by adoptive parents can guide others who are considering adoption or those who have adopted and are still exploring the adoptive parenting role. This book also offers a snapshot of how different families are formed and reveals how adoptive and biological parents are more alike than different."

Jayashree Mohanty, PhD
Assistant Professor
Department of Social Work
National University of Singapore

"I must congratulate everyone who has worked on this book. Just as *Our Very Own* has helped create awareness on the topic of adoption and educated many on where to find help and support in being adoptive parents, I believe *Our Very Own 2* will similarly offer hope and inspiration to adoptees as well as adoptive parents. It is a great resource for anyone who is looking for such locally produced materials.

I am personally touched by an adoptive father who wrote that he was motivated to adopt after an orphanage director shared that 'God made families, not institutions, to look after children'.

Whatever the motivation or reason for adopting or fostering a child, every family in this book has shown that it was love, patience, commitment and sacrifice that saw them through the initial years. For those who shared their stories five years ago in the first book, we now have the privilege of sharing their joys and victories as they reveal how they overcome periods of doubts and challenges.

Our Very Own 2 shows us what true humanity looks like. It shows us what happens when we value, treasure and treat every life with dignity, and see every child as a precious gift from God. Every society needs organisations like TOUCH Adoption Services so that, in addition to helping every family find a child, we will also be able to help find a family for every child."

Jason Wong
Board Chairman
Focus on the Family

CONTENTS

Foreword..ix

Message..xi

Part 1: Decisions... 1

1. Waiting For Our Baby *by Thomas Choi*
   and Lee Pei Lu... 3

2. Laying The Foundation *by Adam and Pauline*........ 8

Part 2: Sequels..15

3. Roots And Shoots *by Lian*................................16

4. Deeper Realisations *by Stuart Frost* 31

5. Letter From Aunt Jenny *shared by Stuart Frost*..... 43

6. Joys Of Wonderment *by Ann Gowing* 49

7. Going Home *by Colin Pereira* 55

8. What If *by Alice* 63

9. Adopting No. 2 *by Low Bee Lian* 68

10. Nursing The Adoption Wound *by Andrea Yee*.......74

Part 3: Adopting From Overseas............................81

11. Growing Our Family *by Ernest Lee and*
    Jin Wang..83

12. The Light At The End Of The Tunnel Is
    Love *by Soo Sing* 94

13. I Choose To Love Her *by The Vass Family*............ 97

Part 4: Destined: Adoptees and Birth Parent Share 109

14. Growing Up Adopted *by Jerome Wong*................ 110

15. I Am Chang Hann *by Chang Hann* 113

16. Letter To My Child *by Birth Mother*..................117

Part 5: Adopting Later In Life 119
   17. Being Older Parents *by Yoke Fong* 121

Part 6: Discoveries 127
   18. Pressure, I Need Pressure *by Jane Samuel* 129
   19. When Your Child Is Out Of Sync *by*
       Laurel Fanning 133

Part 7: Why Not Foster 141
   20. A Fostering Journey *by Lynette Chiu* 142

Part 8: From The Professionals 147
   21. Merging Hearts With Hope And Love
       by Wong Wei Lei 148
   22. Poignant Reflections *by Teo Seok Bee* 151

Part 9: What You Need To Know About Adoption 159

FOREWORD

P eople adopt for many different reasons. The stories in this volume show the different routes to adoption. Whatever the reason, the underlying thread that binds these stories together is love – unconditional love.

This is the kind of love that makes a parent tirelessly carry a crying baby for hours at night, pace anxiously for hours at the hospital as they await the diagnosis for their sick child and endure endless "Why?" questions.

It may surprise some that couples would be willing to do all this (and more!) for a child who is not their biological offspring. Some regard adoption as a noble sacrifice on the part of the adoptive parents, and think that the child who has been adopted is so blessed.

However, in reality, it is the adoptive parents who also find their lives are blessed and enriched by their adopted children. Time and time again, as these stories show, adoptive parents share how fortunate they are to have adopted a child, and what a blessing he/she has been to them. That child becomes *their* child.

My wife looks ethnically Chinese although she is half-Chinese and half-Caucasian. When she was a young girl, she and her mother (who is Caucasian) used to get puzzled stares whenever they went out. Shop assistants would whisper "she must be adopted" as they walked past.

Having experienced this personally, we can fully understand how awkward it must be for parents of adopted children when they have to deal with such insensitive remarks. In this book, parents share useful tips and practical coping mechanisms on how to handle such encounters. Combined with a good sense of humour, their advice will go a long way in helping adoptive parents tackle issues related to adopting a child.

Interestingly, some issues are common to all parents across the board, not just for adoptive families. Take for instance, bonding with your child. The best investment that any parent can make in this process is spending time (and still more time) with their child. This truth applies to both adoptive parents and biological parents.

I respect all the parents (and children) who willingly laid bare the most intimate details of their lives for this book. Thank you for sharing such personal stories with us. We are privileged to have read your testimonies. I hope many people will be as inspired by these stories as I have been.

Christopher de Souza
Member of Parliament
Holland – Bukit Timah GRC
Singapore

MESSAGE

Families are the bedrock of all societies. Whilst some families are formed quite naturally, others are formed uniquely and intentionally through adoption. Adoption is an act of love. Adoption is about providing a family for a child.

This book, a sequel to *Our Very Own* launched in 2010, is a compilation of heartfelt stories written by all whose lives have been touched by adoption – adoptive parents, adopted children, birth parents and adoption workers. In this book, you will read poignant accounts of fears overcome, losses grieved, wounds healed, lives celebrated and families transformed. A common journey, but different stories. Different perspectives but a common thread of love and hope.

Our Very Own 2 also contains the sequel to some of the stories found in *Our Very Own*, chronicling the journey of growth and discovery of adoptive parents and their children, as depicted befittingly by the bigger pair of feet on the book cover. This book intentionally features a story on fostering, a journey that is less trodden. If adoption is about providing a family for a child, then fostering is about being the family for a child for a reason and season. In *Our Very Own 2*, you will also discover the first-hand experiences of adoption workers through two of our long-serving staff, Teo Seok Bee and Wong Wei Lei as they share their personal stories of walking alongside birth and adoptive families in their journeys of pain and joy, healing and fulfilment.

I would like to thank the families who have so generously contributed their stories. Thank you for letting others glimpse into your families, your lives and your hearts. To those who are considering adoption and to those who have adopted, may you be inspired and empowered. To the birth parents who have made the difficult decision of placing your children for adoption, may these stories be an encouragement and affirmation to you.

And to the rest of you, may you be touched by the stories as they have touched mine.

Eugene Seow, PBM
Executive Director
TOUCH Family Services

PART 1

DECISIONS

Thomas and Pei Lu with their 25-month-old daughter whom they adopted soon after sharing their story in this book.

1

Waiting For Our Baby

Thomas Choi and Lee Pei Lu

"We feel you are somewhere, but we have to wait for you to find us."

When one of my colleagues wanted to find out more about adoption in Singapore, I (Pei Lu) immediately thought of my friends James and Simone, who had recently adopted a child through TOUCH Adoption Services. Having gone through the process themselves, naturally they would be the best people to advise my colleague.

So I brought my friends together for a visit. As Simone shared with us about her exciting adoption journey, her joyfulness left a deep impression on me. Unbeknownst to me, that conversation had deposited a seed and sparked a stirring deep within my heart.

Three years later, my husband and I visited James and Simone again – but this time, it was not for a colleague's sake. This time, we were there to find out more about adoption for ourselves.

The afternoon we spent with James and Simone was very significant to us. Thomas and I were deeply touched by their sincere sharing and their acknowledgement of the struggles we were going through.

Having walked the journey themselves, they understood that most couples considering adoption inevitably experienced feelings of unease and uncertainty. We will always remember James saying to us, "May I suggest that you go ahead with all of the required paperwork and see what happens from there?"

Drawn by the same desire to become parents, James and Simone prayed with us before we left.

Riding The Rollercoaster

Shortly after, we took James' suggestion and got going with the adoption application.

Throughout the process, the journey was like a rollercoaster ride as we swung from one end of the emotional pendulum to the other. At times, Thomas was more ready than I, and at other times, I was the one who was more ready. It felt as if our hearts had been turned inside out and upside down!

Despite the turmoil, we made it a point to share our thoughts and feelings honestly with each other and supported each other through prayer. We drew strength from our families and church friends. Day by day, slowly but surely, we found ourselves taking a firmer step towards our goal to becoming parents.

When we finally completed our Home Study Report*, we paid another visit to James and Simone again. They shared with us the changes and challenges they faced after their son, Ignatius, came home. They also expressed the indescribable joy of finally being parents and reminded us that bringing up a child is a privilege that is not granted to everyone.

Before we left, they invited us to peep at three-year-old Ignatius who was taking his nap. The minute I entered the room, my heart was flooded with peace and joy. It was an affirming moment I will not forget.

Along the way to adoption, we read the book ***Our Very Own**: Stories Celebrating Adoptive Families*. The testimonies struck a chord with us. We also attended the Pre-Adoption and Adoption Disclosure Workshops at TOUCH Adoption Services and watched a Japanese movie *Like Father, Like Son*. It was about how a father had to make a life-changing decision to choose his birth son or the boy he had raised after discovering the boys had been switched at birth.

The movie, among other events, further strengthened the conviction in our hearts. Thomas and I became even surer than ever of this path toward parenthood.

---

* *Home Study Report: A Home Study Report is a comprehensive investigation and assessment of the prospective adopters' readiness and suitability to adopt. A Home Study is conducted by professional social service staff from voluntary welfare organisations accredited by the Ministry of Social and Family Development (MSF) in Singapore (https://app.adoption.gov.sg/ ApplyForHomeStudy.aspx).*

We Are Waiting For You

At the Pre-Adoption briefing with TOUCH Adoption Services, I remember vividly what the speaker, an adoptive mom herself, said: "You have to wait for your baby to find you."

Yes indeed, to our yet-to-be-known child, we feel you are somewhere, but we have to wait for you to find us!

We have not yet met you, but we have already started window-shopping in the baby section. Although we should only be browsing, we ended up buying you something each time. We tried to imagine what colour or designs you would like, and it felt amazing to do so.

Although we are not particularly artistic or creative, we bought a scrapbook and some materials. We are waiting for you to kick off the first page and are sure it will be a wonderful life book just for our family.

We have been talking about you to your cousins too. Already, they are excited about your arrival and keep asking when you will be coming.

Where are you, my baby? Are you safe? Is anyone taking care of you? Who comforts you when you cry?

We have been praying: "Abba Father, please keep our baby safe. Deliver our baby from danger. Grant our baby good health, sound sleep and be his/her source of comfort. Your ways are higher than our ways. Your timing is never too soon nor too late. You will arrange the perfect time to bring our family together."

My child, having you is not by chance nor by accident. Your place in this life and family has all been arranged and prepared for a while now.

Thank you for choosing us to be your parents. We cannot wait to meet you!

"The LORD Almighty has sworn, 'Surely, as I have planned, so it will be, and as I have purposed, so it will happen'" (Isaiah 14:24, NIV).

2

Laying The Foundation

Adam and Pauline

"…if we work towards laying a foundation for a relationship that is grounded in trust and transparency, then things will fall in place."

The exact moment is etched in my memory forever. It was 2:45 pm on 16 November 2014. As I was sitting at my desk in the office, intensely working on an important presentation, my handphone rang.

At first, I was inclined to reject the call so as not to disrupt my task at hand. But something prompted me to pick it up.

We were already familiar with TOUCH Adoption Services, having worked closely with them to prepare for our Home Study Report a year ago. So when the caller said she was calling from TOUCH, I sensed something big was in the works.

Destiny On The Line

In hindsight, that phone call was not just any call – it was my destiny calling and there was no way I would have missed it for anything in the world.

As it turns out, there was a potential match of a 10-month-old baby girl for us, but it was still too early to confirm anything. It was a "don't get your hopes up just yet" kind of call to find out if we were interested.

We definitely were! My wife Pauline and I had been waiting eagerly to hear those words for over a year now. Externally, we had gone about our lives as normally as we could, but internally, it had been an emotional rollercoaster. From hope and yearning to impatience to mental resolve, all the spectrum of emotions ebbed and flowed within us every day.

At that moment, when I picked up that phone call, all those emotions came to a standstill. After a few cursory questions, I said, "Yes".

The first thing I did after I hung up was to call Pauline to tell her the news. My mind was racing with excitement and apprehension. To this day, I have no idea what happened to that important presentation I had been working on!

The next few days were a mad rush of frenzied activity and decision-making. It was by far the biggest decision we had to make as a couple. It was critical to keep our senses about us and not succumb to the emotional enormity of the event.

We found an extremely helpful partner in TOUCH Adoption Services whose staff hand-held us through the entire process. They guided us on both the practical and emotional fronts, making sure we did not feel overwhelmed while ensuring we covered the legal bases and keeping us fully aware of what to expect at each step.

Love Arrived In An Instant

Exactly four days after that fateful phone call, little Nora was sleeping with us on our bed! Within hours, we had totally fallen in love with her.

There is a reason why nature allows a nine-month gestational period for the human species. Besides the obvious reasons of biological growth, this timeframe is crucial for parents to mentally prepare for a new member to live amongst them and come to terms with the fact that their lives will never be the same again.

While most parents had nine months, Pauline and I only had *four days* to prepare. Hence, it was head-first into on-the-job-training for us. We were determined to get it right from the start. The pre- and post-adoption talks that we attended, along with literature about adoptive parenting, gave us some key insights on how to proceed.

The first few months were as much as an adjustment for Nora as much as it was for us. Even though she was not able to articulate her feelings at that age, the sudden change in her environment would certainly have had a big impact on her.

As such, we focused on getting two key things right:

* Providing A Comfortable Environment

Our first priority was to create a physically familiar and comfortable environment for Nora, so that she would not feel too displaced from her known surroundings.

To do this, we did our best to learn about her habits and daily routine from her birth family and tried to replicate as much of those as possible. This included her favourite foods, toys and music. We also placed her pictures around the house and started using some of the baby words she relied on to express herself. We wanted to show her that she could still communicate in familiar ways.

For my wife and I, this meant our daily lives had completely changed in an instant! Of course, we could not have been happier and considered ourselves fortunate to even have this opportunity.

* Building Unbreakable Bonds

We also recognised the importance of creating an immediate bond with her, as that would lay the foundation for our relationship in the future.

"Bonding time" became the most important part of the day. As the mother, my wife naturally took the lead in this, but I believe that the father also has a critical role to play in making this new and wonderful relationship work.

Given Nora's age, verbal communication was not an option, so the entire process had to be done behaviourally where she "felt" the bond more than she "understood" it. My wife (who took an extended period off from work) spent almost the entire day with Nora, taking care of her and essentially becoming the most familiar person in her life.

I, on the other hand, was her designated "fun partner", ensuring that our time together was active and entertaining. We made the most of evenings and weekends. There was a different activity planned for each day, involving toys, colouring books, photo-taking sessions, playground activities and outdoor strolls.

Nora showed a special fascination for the swimming pool at an early age and thus the kiddie pool became our regular haunt. My personal favourite bonding time with her was when I prepared her for bedtime – 20 minutes every evening, carrying her, hugging her and singing lullabies until she fell asleep. Very soon, through the physical presence and the amount of time spent together, our little family started experiencing a shared state-of-mind and feelings of joy.

Creating New Memories

Six months later, we settled into a routine in our personal and social life with Nora. Being an adoptive parent is a blessing that few have a chance to experience, and Pauline and I are thankful to be counted amongst those.

The people around us – family, friends and partners (such as the staff at TOUCH Adoption Services) – play a very crucial role in determining the initial success of this life-changing event. However, at the end of the day, it ultimately boils down to the parents and the child to make this work, with the greater onus being on the parents.

A part of the secret lies in having unshakeable faith in the bond that has been created – one that is not defined by biology (nature) but rather, by nurture. This includes nurturing a sense of belonging and the ageless human spirit of kinship.

For our little family, we have just embarked on this incredible journey, which (I hope) will last a lifetime. We will certainly face challenges and pitfalls, as every family does (I am told that the tough questions start when the child hits three), but if we work towards laying a foundation for a relationship that is grounded in trust and transparency, then things will fall into place.

Through all of this, we must not forget to have fun and create happy memories as we go along. This entire experience has been an incredible blessing and we count every moment as a gift. We intend to plan for the future while cherishing the present.

In the words of master Oogway, from the Kung Fu Panda series: "Yesterday is history, tomorrow is a mystery, today is a gift – that is why it is called the present".

We most certainly got our present – our little Nora.

PART 2
SEQUELS

3

Roots And Shoots

Lian

"Did I cry, mom, when she left me?"

Whenever the issue of your identity arises, so many different scenes of you in different environments rush into my mind. How can I simply put you in one box?

I picture you, my then seven-year-old, staring out of a car window, rain pelting down, a grey fog covering the rice fields in Loudi, China, the city of your birth. Your eyes strain to look as you ask:

"Mom, where are all the Chinese people?"

Then I see you standing on a mountain pass in Northern Vietnam, as the Hmong people, with whom you identified, come and go in the marketplace. You fling your arms open, declaring:

"I love being in China!"

I see you standing on a staircase asking for "aah-scream", my Southern Hemisphere accent coming through in a word that you learnt from me.

All too frequently now, I see you, my 15-year-old of today, all dressed up with your friends, ready to hit the town, throwing back your head and exclaiming at some joke in your proper British accent.

Who are you, this daughter of mine?

Where are you from?

Where are you going?

Years ago, a prompting to discover your roots inspired our return to the land of your birth on what is called a "heritage" tour. The time was right. You had just turned seven and, as was our usual custom, I was telling you the story of the night of your birth (as had been told to me by the officials) while we lay together in the half-light.

Like so many moms, I was expecting identity issues to surface, but I was unprepared for just how dramatic that moment would be.

That night, for the first time, you asked a different set of questions:

"Did I cry, mom, when she left me?"

"I don't know." (Rule No. 1: Never tell a lie when the truth will do.)

"Does Mama Lou know?" (referring to the director of the Welfare Centre, whom I had affectionately called "Mama Lou")

"But when did my mom put me in her arms?"

"She did not put you in her arms."

"Then whose arms?"

(Moment of truth!) "She put you down in the courtyard where she knew you would be found."

"She left me?"

I nod, perilously close to tears.

"But how, mom? How could she?"

Your voice is a thick whisper. For the first time since I have known you, your face is etched in grief. My tears spill over as I scoop you up in my arms and cry.

"I don't know, but this I do know – I will never do that to you. I will never let you go. You are mine forever. We are forever family."

The Next Step

In the days and weeks thereafter, all was calm as this pebble slowly rippled out and into your seven-year-old consciousness. Then, when you were ready, the request came:

"Mom, can we go to China?"

I had waited for this moment. It was time.

Through our online group of adoptive parents, I found Terry, a facilitator in China. I was thrilled. It would be just us! This meant that everything would be tailored to our mission. I made the requests and Terry set up everything. This was your BIG adventure, but I felt so safe.

Terry was so solicitous, right down to the last detail! She even arranged for us to stay at the same hotel where we had been for your adoption. Six years later, everything had become bigger, smoother and more commercialised. Nothing was the same anymore…

The special floor that had been set aside for adoptive parents was no longer there and the little baby shop where we had bought your first pair of shoes was also gone. The restaurant where we had dined the night before meeting you was now a busy local eatery.

A sense of loss and nostalgia washed over me, but I reminded myself that what mattered now was the fact that here you were, with me.

Walking Into The Past

The next morning, on the four-hour drive to the birth city, Terry played traditional games with you to keep you entertained. I was still somewhat anxious.

What would we find?

What would you think?

How would you feel?

How would I manage?

Finally, the seven hills, which gave the city its name, were before us. (Actually, it is only six hills now. The seventh hill had been excavated as the city was expanding.) This number was symbolic, for each of the years you had been with us.

That wet Sunday afternoon, we drove around the city. You had your window open, so the rain fell on you, but you were oblivious. I, too, had my nose pressed against the glass, peering out into the gloom. I knew who I was trying to find – your birth mother! As if I could recognise her – perhaps a grown-up version of you?

Seven years later, as we talked about this chapter I was writing, you informed me:

"Mom, when we were driving round that day, you know what I was looking for? My mom! It's weird, isn't it?"

No, just us, I think!

You walked into your past as we stepped out of the lift the next morning. You were wearing your crushed velvet and lace pink dress. With your inimitable flair, you had topped the outfit off with your pink floral lace-up boot sneakers!

Two women and two men were seated on a sofa. I recognised three of them – Mama Lou, her accountant and the driver. They were all there at our beginning. The other man was the regional government official, posted to ensure that we stuck to the script and took home a good impression of the Motherland.

The woman seated in the middle saw you and opened her arms – and you ran into them! You, who were always wary of strangers! Mama Lou crooned over you. Everyone exclaimed, holding you at arm's length to examine the beautiful person that you are.

Reunited with Mama Lou for the first time after your adoption.

Mama Lou formally welcomed you home. We, your parents, were forgotten as you headed out with them into their van. Was this really you, who just last year, could not bear to be separated from me?

We drove into the courtyard of the welfare centre. A girl with Down's Syndrome sat and watched. The building was small and shabby; dark green paint flaked from the walls; the passages were empty and dark. Apparently, it used to be an old office, which had been hastily converted into a welfare centre, when people began to leave their babies at the Central Affairs Bureau, which was located at the entrance to the courtyard in which we now stood.

Upstairs in Mama Lou's office, we were plied with platters of fruit. Our facilitator Terry was worth her weight in gold. Yes, this very room was the room in which you had slept!

Presents were exchanged and Mama Lou graciously received your little hand-drawn booklet and the printed bound book we had prepared showing your life story since your adoption, including your world travels and what made you a "third culture kid".

We asked to see your file and Terry was permitted to view this. There was nothing new to learn as Mama Lou regretfully explained that they had not been required to keep documents until recently.

Filling A Hole

Suddenly, at the sound of a baby's cry, Mama Lou dashed out to deal with an emergency. You followed.

When we caught up with you, you were in the next room, standing over a baby who had been left overnight with hydrocephalus. A tube with a bag of liquid was attached to the baby's head. The baby's hand was curled around your finger.

I could not help but think that something in you must have known what this felt like, to be left alone, in an unfamiliar setting. This was why you had come – to be with her, to fill a hole in her heart.

The doctor attends to the new arrival, with you helping.

We wandered around the premises, no other children in sight. The older children, with limited chances of adoption, were at school. Yes, there was the tiled bathroom with the small round plastic bowl in which you were bathed. You had a panic attack that first night when we put you in a big bath!

There was the doctor, who came to assist us when you developed a cold in the hotel. The bunk beds bought with the money raised by our online adoption parent group were there too!

You were plied with food at the lunch banquet organised by Mama Lou, who fed you with her own chopsticks. At the new American store, we bought trainers for all the children as our gift to the welfare centre.

Mama Lou spent the entire afternoon playing with you. You got up close and personal, pulling each other's cheeks, ruffling each other's hair, laughing and whooping, as if you had never been apart. I watched her closely and felt so thankful for this big-hearted woman.

Mama Lou thought that I was jealous!

Oh Mama Lou, my heart was so filled with gratitude to you for being so caring and making this homecoming so special for my daughter! You were truly filling a hole in my daughter's heart!

We went to see the site of the new welfare centre, built to house vulnerable children and the elderly. It was located on the outskirts of the city near the big copycat marble "White House", which were the home of the new municipal offices.

The rain had turned the ground into a muddy clay mire. Mama Lou scooped you on her back and carried you over this terrain, her own office shoes caked in the red wet clay.

Mama Lou carries you across the muddy grounds.

Just when we were ready to say goodbye and thank you, Mama Lou apologised for not being able to spend the next morning with us, but she asked if she could teach you to play badminton in the afternoon. Yes?

At the middle school we visited, you did not like being surrounded by so many children and you held my hand tightly.

Finding The Real Truth

The next morning, we stopped at the Civil Affairs Bureau that stood at the entrance to the courtyard in which the current welfare centre sat.

Unusually, we were permitted to visit with the man who had found you.

Unusually, we had his name on your "Abandonment" Certificate, or what I preferred to call your "Safe and Found" Certificate.

According to Terry, the government official was so delighted with the course of the visit thus far and the establishment of international relationships that he had agreed. I mean, what could go wrong?

A tall attractive man came out of the small office to meet us and welcomed us inside, where an equally tall woman was waiting. You looked good with them. Gifts were exchanged. Snatches of the conversation squeezed painfully at my heart.

The family who found you.

"Found in the courtyard at night… sounded like a wounded animal… two young people jumped on a motorcycle when we picked her up… New padded suit, red… taken to the hospital across the road… every second day for 10 days… pipes to help her to breathe… kept here with us and our two children… wanted her… took her to work with me, she never wanted to be set down, clung to me… not permitted to keep her, so after three months, given to the welfare centre… wife visited her every day. Yes, there was a note, with her birthdate, yes we handed this to the officials… Yes, please keep in contact, here are our family's contact details (the names, ages and contact numbers were provided for all four members)."

The government official had slipped out during this conversation and taken you with him. This was a very different story to the sanitised version that we had been given on Adoption Day.

I wanted to stay, but there was nothing more to say. Your second father handed over a *hong bao* (red packet) for you.

Once outside, I looked: *A month's wages!*

My mind was whirling. I tasked Terry to return this as courteously as possible. She was gone for a long time. When she returned, Terry told us that he had refused to take the money back. He was concerned that you were being ill-treated, as your skin was tanned. He stated that he had wanted to give you so much when you were a baby and could not, but now he and his wife were both earning good wages and their two children were away at university.

We drove away in silence. Questions hurled down the corridors of my mind. Who was this family, really? Why would they care so much? Would we ever know?

At the police station where your "finding" as a baby had been reported, you were more interested in playing a game with Terry on the grass.

Meanwhile, my heart was overflowing. You had been so loved! Yet you had been left. No wonder it had been so hard for you to trust "forever"!

This was hard for me! How much harder it must have been for you!

God's Care Along The Way

Back at the hotel, I lay on the bed with you and shared just a little of the new information I had found out that day. I wanted you to know how God took care of you and placed people along your path to protect you as a baby – and how He always will.

I enumerated each protector. I was aching inside for you and my heart broke for everything you had to take on board. Smart as a whip, you responded:

"Wow, so you are Mama No. 4, but don't worry, mama, you go to the top of the list!"

Still, there was no time then to think this through. We had to go for our badminton lesson with Mama Lou. Her minions spent the entire afternoon running after shuttlecocks while Mama Lou patiently taught you how to play badminton.

Mama Lou teaches you to play badminton.

That evening, we hosted a banquet to say thank you to Mama Lou. She ceremonially handed you a beautifully carved jade goblet and then instructed a staff member to give you her necklace when you admired it!

The next morning, we watched the funeral procession of a high-ranking hospital official, complete with firecrackers and all, as staff in white lined the road in the softly falling rain. This was a fitting end to our homecoming trip.

Downstairs, Mama Lou was waiting for us. She looked very solemn and sad as she handed you a coffee-table picture book of the city of your birth. She asked you to come home often. She told you that for many years, she had not allowed herself to feel, as she had had to give away so many children. Yet, she said you had opened up her heart again.

You and Mama Lou hug one last time. Our hearts were full.

This had been a rollercoaster ride, but there is still one more stop to go.

We returned with the government official to the building where you had been adopted. It was silent now. But I so well remembered that day when I took you in my arms, held you, claimed you and made you mine.

* * * * * *

It has been eight years now since that trip. Whenever we sit and talk about that time, you say you can hardly recall, although you tell me that with your visual memory, you remember pictures, not emotions.

You tell me that you are "fine" now – that this is your past and what is important is our life together now.

Perhaps that is what that journey did for you. It allowed you to fill that gaping hole with pictures, and now that you have memories, you can move on.

You have embraced who you are now.

You have embraced who *we* are now.

That is what counts. Roots have allowed you to grow shoots.

This is the sequel to the story "This Is To Mother You" first published in Our Very Own (2010).

4

Deeper Realisations

Stuart Frost

"To the birth mothers of 'our' children, I thank you from the bottom of my heart and pledge to keep my promise to look after them."

It has been several years since the release of *Our Very Own* in 2010. Our family has moved on; Jay is now nine years old and Vik is eight. Our heads ruled our hearts and we did not adopt a third child. How time flies; how I am sounding more like my parents every day!

Our friends and family have been wonderful with our children. When my parents read *Our Very Own*, they were surprised there was no mention of grandparents. I guess it is all too common to take our parents and their support network for granted; in fact, I am starting to understand that one myself, now that I have become a parent too.

Some grandparents have an issue with their children adopting; luckily, this is not so with my parents. I am very happy that they are still with us and in relatively good health, even in their 70s. It is great that they are a part of the boys' lives as children learn a lot from positive interaction with their grandparents.

This also helps to bind the family together whilst teaching them to see life from another angle.

Mom and dad, apologies for the omission in the last book and thank you for everything!

They Know More Than You Think

Modern-day adoption practices advocate early disclosure to children, which we have done with our kids and are very comfortable with it.

As I watch my children grow, I am beginning to further understand what it means to be a parent and how the child deserves to know the truth, even though this may cause some issues.

We try hard to get the balance right; being adopted will be one of the segments of their self-definition. However, we hope that this will not be disproportionate.

Over the past couple of years, there have been some interesting moments with our kids.

For example, when Jay was about six or seven years old, he went through a stage asking if he could meet his birth mother. We told him we would definitely try to do that when he was older, but we would need to talk it through beforehand.

He asked why he had to be older. We explained that it was a bit complicated and now was not the best time, but that we were there for him. The kicker came when he said:

"But she will be dead by the time I am older!"

"Well, why would you think that?" I asked, hiding my surprise.

Jay looked me in the eye and said, "She has white hair already, you know."

"Come on, Jay, how would you know that? You're bluffing me."

He just smiled.

This was a bit of a shock and we did our best to handle the situation. We asked him how he could possibly know that. He just grinned cheekily at us. He knew he was just making it up, even if there was a concern that he might not meet her one day.

Being Upfront

Thankfully, the times we had spent with TOUCH Adoption Services (TAS) and TOUCH Adoptive Families Network (TAFNET) during the adoption process, Pre-Adoption, Disclosure Workshops and various adoption seminars TAS organized really helped us to prepare for situations like this. We knew we had to be flexible and accept that this type of discussion would be a normal part of our parent/child relationship.

Since *Our Very Own* was published in 2010, Jay has entered primary school. Last year, we went for parent/teacher interviews. During the discussion, we felt we should mention that he was an adopted child, just in case situations might arise in class, as it is obvious from physical appearances that I could not be his biological father since I am a Caucasian (British). (My wife is third-generation Indian Sikh, and the boys are both Indian, adopted from Malaysia.)

This fact was later mentioned in the classroom. It turns out that his teacher was an adoptive mother too and completely understood. There was a connection of understanding between us, not only of our own experiences, but also the journey that our children would go through. Perhaps adoption is not so rare after all.

Who Is My Tummy Mummy?

My second son Vik is more reticent to discuss his adoption story. Once, he asked my wife, "Could it have been that you would not be my mummy?".

My wife had to take a breath and tell him (or "admit", as she says) that this might well have been the case. It is possible that he might have been born to another tummy mummy or adopted into a different household, but what was important was that we have each other and our family, and that we are all here for each other.

On another occasion, Vik inquired again about his tummy mummy. Jay then asked why his tummy mummy gave him away and did not want him.

My wife gently explained that it was not that his tummy mummy did not want him necessarily, but that her situation meant she might not have had much choice in the matter. She then steered the conversation away and talked about how happy we have been adopting them instead.

We think this is a good way of dealing with these questions. Like all parents, we are not 100 percent sure and are just trying our best. Hopefully this is not something that negatively sticks in their minds. Perhaps my sons can read this book when they are older and understand our situation better!

No Explanation Needed

As we have adopted interracially, we still get quite a few comments, typically a confused "This is your son?", accompanied by quizzical looks.

At first, I was not sure how to handle it as I had not had any experience with such a situation. Should you reveal that your kids are adopted? Are you going to have to do that all the time, for the next 20 years? You cannot gush every time that your child is adopted and come across sounding like you are justifying the situation.

Now I am so used to it, I just say, "Yes, he is my son."

There is no indecision and I feel only pride. If someone is confused, it really is not my issue. I have to think of my kids, and not concern myself with explaining the history to a stranger.

When looking at our second son, a lot of people say, "Ah yes, I can see he looks like you both."

We usually smile and nod, then look at each other whilst laughing hard on the inside. It has become like a standing private joke between me and my wife.

I guess some people like to pigeon-hole everyone in life. That is OK, it can be amusing.

When Realisation Dawns

In *Our Very Own*, I shared the story of how, at the age of 13, my mother told me about my grandfather not being my "real blood" grandfather (not my terminology). In the book, I discussed what it meant to me and how, from this, I knew I could adopt.

When my mother read the book, she reminded me that the family had always told me about my grandfather even before I was 13. It was just that, on that particular day, I had simply understood what it meant, whereas previously I did not fully comprehend the situation. It was as if I had an "aha" moment of realisation at that point in time.

This revelation by my own mother shows me that although we can be honest and tell our kids about their adoption story, they may not fully understand it just yet. It may be much later in their lives when they have their own "aha" moments of realisation and start to comprehend what being adopted really means.

When this realisation dawns, it might either cause some angst or there might be a smooth acceptance with no issues. Whichever the case, our job is to support them patiently.

Central to our identity and psychological security is knowing where we had come from, namely, our parents. Unless we have been adopted ourselves, we cannot appreciate what it means to have physically come from someone we do not know.

As adoptive parents, we feel our responsibility is to try and equip our kids as best as possible to handle their adoption journeys. My father has always told me that parents have a fiduciary responsibility, in the fullest and widest sense of the word, towards their children.

I cannot agree more. How things have changed between my father and I since my teenage years. How happy I am he is still with me to witness my journey into parenthood, and how thankful I am to him for keeping a straight face!

No Two Stories Are Alike

Reflecting on what life might bring for my children and the excellent work TAS and TAFNET do to assist all adoption stakeholders bring two stories to mind.

The first is about John, one of my parents' neighbours, who is in his 60s. Upon hearing that we had adopted the boys, he revealed that he was an adoptee too. However, he said he had never had any interest in finding his birth parents and that he was content with his life and the adoptive home he had grown up in.

In contrast to this, the second story is about my godmother Aunt Jenny (my mother's cousin) who lives in England. An only child and an adoptee herself, she is now over 60 years old and has shared some of her experiences with us. I am not sure if it has been interesting or difficult in any way for her to see us go through modern-day adoption with our two boys.

At the age of five, on her first day at school, Jenny's mother told her that she was adopted. There had been no preparation, no adoption story and no TAS to assist. She went off to school completely bewildered. Until now, she still remembers that traumatic day clearly.

Making Contact

Fast-forward 50 years, Aunt Jenny has her own son who is now 35 years old. About 15 years ago, she decided to attempt to find her birth mother. What motivated her to do so was because she thought her son might want to know his genetic origins. She asked her adoptive parents for their input, and they agreed.

In the United Kingdom, there is a national agency designated for adoption stakeholders who want to find their birth families. There are strict guidelines; people have to write to the agency and they will only progress the situation if both sides have written in to pro-actively seek contact.

Upon Aunt Jenny's enquiry, the agency responded, informing her that for decades, a letter from her birth mother had been in their files. Contact was facilitated and Jenny discovered that she was her mother's firstborn. In fact, her birth mother had gone on to marry her birth father and had several more children. That means that not only was Aunt Jenny the firstborn, but she also had siblings! Her son was the eldest grandchild.

The contact progressed from writing (where the handwriting was uncannily similar) to telephone calls and subsequently, a face-to-face meeting which involved both her adoptive and birth parents.

Quite naturally, the facial features were similar too, including hair and eye colour. Yet, my aunt told me she was overwhelmed and felt that something was still missing. She eventually spoke to a counsellor and in the process, discovered (a realisation!) that certain areas of her life had been governed and ruled by her adoption experience.

Something Deeper Inside

Through counselling, Aunt Jenny acquired a book on adoption which she lent to me, titled *The Primal Wound** by Nancy Verrier. I was shocked upon reading it as I found much of it to be upsetting.

The book alludes to a wound that just cannot be healed, no matter what is done, but it can only be coped with. It distressed me to read that my sons (and other innocent children) might have emotional baggage to carry throughout their lives which is no fault of their own.

Not being an adoptee myself, I would not know if what was written was fair, but she told me she identified strongly with it. The book described a common occurrence whereby adoptees felt that a piece of the jigsaw was missing but when it was finally found, it did not fit.

Obviously, her parents would never have wanted her to feel that way. It is terribly sad, however, and I am hoping that the way we approach adoption with the guidance of TAS and support of TAFNET might help to minimise such feelings for our children in the future.

On a happier note, my aunt lives a successful and fulfilling life. She has a very close relationship with her son and is still in contact with her birth family, although it is not perfect. I emailed my aunt to ask her permission to print this paragraph. What I received in reply is in the next chapter (included with

---

* *Verrier, Nancy, "The Primal Wound: Understanding the Adopted Child", Verrier Publishing, 2003.*

her permission), which offers an amazing insight into my aunt's specific journey as well as the mind of an adoptee.

You Have Our Word

As I think about my children's birth mothers. I feel connected to them through "our" sons. I hope they are doing well and I wonder how often they think about their children.

As the boys get older and I see their characters develop, I wonder how their lives would have turned out if they had not been adopted. As they grow up, I see the importance of the fiduciary responsibility mentioned earlier, but also an additional responsibility towards my sons' birth mothers.

When Jay's birth mother first saw us, she told one of the interpreters that she was happy about the situation because she said she could see that we were a good couple.

What a conclusion to make within three minutes of seeing us and not a word spoken!

We insisted on letting her know through the interpreter that we promised to love and care for her son and he would be well looked after. We might never know the extent of the pain the birth mothers experienced when deciding to place their children for adoption, but to us, the recipients, it has been the most precious "gift" we could ask for in life.

Ironically, I do not feel the same way about the fathers. Perhaps it is because we never met them or that we do not know their story. Or perhaps they did not carry the children to term and were not involved in the adoption decision or do not even know they are the biological fathers of my children.

To the birth mothers of "our" children, I thank you from the bottom of my heart and pledge to keep my promise to look after them. You can count on my word.

This is the sequel to the story "Inexplicable Love" first published in Our Very Own (2010).

5

Letter From Aunt Jenny

Shared by Stuart Frost

"Love stitched this family together."

Hi Stuart,

I was very interested to hear about how you and the boys are dealing with the obvious situations that will occur, due to their adoption. It sounds to me that you are doing a great job. It cannot be easy, now that both Jay and Vik are getting older and can begin to comprehend what adoption means. They will start to ask questions!

Having been in that situation as an adoptee, their questions serve two purposes: First, to find out as much as possible about where they had come from; and second, to seek and receive reassurance from their adoptive parents about their own security.

They want to know that their parents love them and will not abandon them, as they may feel their birth parents had done.

In my situation, having been adopted in England in the early 1950s, it was not possible to have any contact with one's birth parents, nor was any information available about them or their family situation. All my adoptive parents and I knew, as far as we were aware, was that my birth mother was still at school and my birth father was in the navy.

My imagination ran riot over the years as to how my birth came about. In addition, I could never get an answer to the burning question of why I was "given away" and "unwanted".

In my teens, when your mind and body are going through confusing times anyway, I found that the best way of dealing with the "not knowing" was to shut it out, be fiercely independent and not rely on others as much as possible. My friends could not comprehend why I was not curious about where I had come from or why I did not want to find my birth parents.

I can honestly say that this strategy got me through life quite well until I became a mother myself. Even then, I only went looking for my birth parents when my son was a teenager and I was in my early 40s. This was because I felt that it may be important for him to find out where he had come from.

In some ways, establishing contact has been a bit like opening Pandora's Box. I would have liked to watch my birth family from afar, without interacting with them. Having taken the lid off the box, sometimes I wish I could put it back on again!

After waiting all those years, although the physical similarities were (illogically) quite a shock, I felt – and still sometimes feel – that we are very different. Despite their wanting me to be closer to them, I do not feel I am able to. I am fine with visiting them where they live, but am still somewhat uncomfortable when they visit me and enter my world. Individually, I do quite enjoy meeting with my biological sisters and brother, but am still glad to return to my own world afterwards.

Somewhere in my subconsciousness, I still have a problem with my birth mother. I feel bad about it, as I know she had no choice but to place me for adoption. Had I not been adopted, I would not have had so many more opportunities in life. But I still cannot help how I feel.

I am also ashamed to admit that, when growing up, I was not as close to or appreciative of my adoptive parents as I wish I had been in hindsight. They were so supportive of me. I always felt loved and knew they were proud of me.

When I decided I should go looking for my birth parents, I discussed it with them first. They could not have been more supportive and fully understood why I felt I should. In fact, on one occasion, they all met up. It was a surreal but positive experience.

As it turned out, my birth parents eventually got married and had three more children. My birth mother expressed her gratitude to my mother for having brought me up and looked after me so well for her, while my mother expressed her gratitude that she had been given the opportunity to bring me up and care for me.

My two fathers got on very well too, and I could see certain similarities in them, both being the laidback sort.

When I met up with them all for the first time, strangely I felt no emotion at all. The years of shutting away my feelings had done their job well. However, a week or so afterwards, I felt this huge rush of emotion and (I am ashamed to admit) anger towards my birth mother.

Happily, I sought post-adoption counselling, which brought several eureka moments where I discovered a reason for the way I had always dealt with life and relationships. For example, never letting anyone get close to me (in case they left, like my mother had done) and testing people who tried to get close by pushing them away (again, to see if they would leave).

There were many other examples, but you get the picture. As you know, I identified greatly with the book *Primal Wound* by Nancy Verrier. It was interesting to note that you thought the book was quite negative, whereas I found it very therapeutic. I guess we are looking at it from different perspectives.

After meeting my birth family, followed by the counselling (and reading that book), I felt much more at peace with myself. I started to come to terms with my past and was able to move forward feeling more of a whole person.

I am no longer overrun by the feelings I described earlier – it is just that when I think about my situation from time to time, I recall that those were the difficulties I encountered. I just wish I had known about the classic characteristic traits of an adopted person back then, so that I could understand why I behaved the way I did and not beat myself up over it.

I do not want you to think I did not have a happy and fulfilled childhood – because I did! I am sure your boys will too. Love, trust, understanding, support and reassurance are the anchors.

I honestly believe that the picture will be much better for Jay and Vik as they have more of the jigsaw puzzle pieces and know more about who they are. They will not have to grow up wondering where they came from. They will be able to understand what has happened to them and know that none of it is their fault.

Your being always open and honest with them will help them a lot. Knowing where they have come from and being assured that they are wanted, loved and cherished will give them confidence going forward.

I apologise for having gone on at length. I just wanted you to understand the whole picture.

Love to you all,
Aunt Jenny

6

Joys Of Wonderment

Ann Gowing

*"As I grieved the deep loss of my womb mother –
the one who created me – suddenly I felt very
much in touch with Jake's possible future grief
over the loss of his womb mother."*

At nearly five years old, Jake has blossomed. He is
cheeky, funny, sporty, sociable, loving, confident,
outgoing, gorgeous, clever, creative, ACTIVE – and
so much more! He is our son, in every way, forever and forever.

I am writing this from our beautiful home in the French Alps
where, as some of you may recall from *Our Very Own,* my first
story was inspired four years ago when we travelled here for the
first time with Jake, then nine months old.

Back then, I was blessed to be here with my husband Adam
and our son Jake.

Today, I feel even more blessed to live here now, immersed in
nature, surrounded by mountains and lakes, with good friends,
a good school, a good life and, more importantly, a healthy son!

When Jake first came to us, we had a very rocky start with his sickness due to an infection that caused an abnormal blood count. I still cry whenever I look at the photos of baby Jake in the hospital – it was a heartbreaking time for us. Those years saw numerous visits to the doctors and hospital – from asthma attacks to a febrile convulsion, eye operation and more!

Thankfully, as many people believed he would, Jake bounced back. In fact, since we moved to France in the summer of 2013, Jake has only visited the doctors once – and that was for the common flu. And no hospitals either!

A Bright Light

Sadly, my mother became very ill in 2013 and I did have to visit her in the hospital in England many times. She passed away in February 2014.

Before she died, I had the chance to thank her for her unwavering belief in Jake. Since that first day he was admitted to the hospital as a baby, she never stopped believing in his recovery. Her support made all the difference.

Mom held onto her belief that he was a fighter and he would be fine. There were days when I would get so depressed that she would say to me, "Ann, he is a tough little fella and he will get through this."

Not only did I thank my mom for her belief in Jake, but I also thanked her again for her overwhelming love and acceptance. She loved him as one of her very own bloodline grandchildren and he was treated no differently than the rest of the family. I know he brought joy and light into her life.

When my dear brother passed away in 2011, Jake brightened up my grieving mom's life with his presence. I knew then how deeply blessed we were that he had become a part of our family.

More recently at a yoga retreat, as I mourned my womb mother's death – the one who created me – suddenly I felt very much in touch with Jake's possible future grief over the loss of his womb mother. I am grateful for this experience and insight as I know it will be of immeasurable value when the time comes.

Asia Is In Our Blood

We had left Singapore in June 2013 to spend those last precious months with my dying mother. After having lived in Singapore for 7 years, we were sad to leave the country.

It also meant leaving behind our hopes and dreams of adopting another child. But we decided it was time to move on and get off the emotional rollercoaster ride that we felt we had been on for years.

Initially, we had very much wanted to expand our family and adopt a girl. However, we were not successful with a second adoption – although we were led to believe, more than once, that we would be matched with a child.

Unfortunately, things did not go our way. The agency we engaged did not communicate with us, and the previous agency that had been so helpful in matching us with Jake told us they were no longer matching local children to expat families (although, later on, we found this was not true).

Since leaving Singapore, the adoption regulations have also changed for British citizens, so all the more, we feel extremely blessed that we have our son.

Having lived and breathed Asia for two decades of my adult life, Asia is in my blood and, of course, it is literally within Jake! Jake knows he is from Singapore and we have a lovely map on his wall to show where Singapore sits within the world – where his birth family lives – and where we live now.

We talk openly to all our friends about how we met Jake and we educate them on what language to use and explain that we are his parents. Both Adam and I have fond hearts for Asia – it will always be a huge part of who we are. I am authentic in how I speak of this love of Asia and Singapore, its land and cultures, and know that Jake will soak up this love from us as well.

In two years, Jake will be about seven years old. We plan to bring him back to visit Singapore and Asia then. At that age, he will be old enough to understand his birthplace and his adoption story.

For now, things could not be better. Of course, as with any parent, there have been times when we have had no map, reference or textbook on how to parent the right way. What has struck me, however, as an adopted parent, is how much more aware we are of how we want to raise our child and what our parenting values are.

We are pleased that another family from Singapore who moved to Switzerland has started an adoptive families support group. This is vital for us – and Jake – that we meet and see other families of different origins and features, as unlike Singapore, our immediate environment in France is not racially diverse.

Presently, Jake has settled very well into French school. He has taken it all in his stride and now bounces into class saying "Bonjour" to his teacher.

We have openly talked to the teachers about Jake's adoption and the fact that when he was growing up, he was about six months behind his peers in major developmental milestones such as walking.

Now, that gap is narrowing and he is superior in many activities compared to his older counterparts, such as cycling without training wheels since age four.

Full Of Love

Both Adam and I revel in watching our son ski, climb trees, swim in lakes, grow his own lettuces and tomatoes, and be surrounded by the natural world. This is what we hold in our deepest values – the love of nature and love of our family.

Every day, we get the most amazing hugs and kisses from Jake. Every night, I watch him sleeping and feel overwhelmed with the love I feel for him – how totally gorgeous, funny and swell he is.

I am proud of the way we have raised Jake and feel that as forever parents, we are ready to support Jake in any way he may need in the future.

We feel very fortunate and grateful for all that we have – namely, our beautiful son Jake. I want to shout from the top of the mountain and tell the world, "Wow! My life is full of love – love for my family and love for the nature that surrounds me!"

This is the sequel to the story "Tears Of Amazement" first published in Our Very Own (2010).

7

Going Home

Colin Pereira

"We have come to realise it is not Sam who is the fortunate one, but us."

As the plane taxied towards the runway at Phnom Penh International Airport, I glanced through the narrow gap between the seats to the row behind me where my wife, Susan was seated next to our son, Sam.

He seemed a bit upset and had a sad look on his face. He spoke to Susan so softly that I could not make out his words over the din of the engine as the plane readied itself for takeoff.

I was curious about what they were talking about, but my attention was soon taken up by our daughter, Christina, who was in an animated state after our long weekend holiday in Cambodia.

It was only several hours later, after we had arrived home in Singapore and the children had been put to bed that I finally got a chance to ask Susan what Sam had been upset about.

"He asked, 'Why did you choose me?'," my wife replied.

It was a poignant question from a six-year-old, but his feelings were understandable after his three-day journey of discovery in the country where he had been born.

Where It All Began

Our fates had intertwined in March 2008 when Susan and I had first visited the Kais Village orphanage in rural Kompong Speu province.

We had embarked on the adoption process five months earlier when we did our Home Study Report in Singapore. In our search for a child, we travelled to Phnom Penh in January, where we met Karen and Sunny, the directors of a non-governmental organisation that managed Kais Village.

Impressed by their dedication to building a sustainable community for orphaned and abandoned children in rural Cambodia, we returned to the country a few months later to see the place for ourselves.

It was an eye-opening visit. We spent several hours mingling and playing with the children in the nursery. With nearly 20 infants there, it was quite difficult to tell them apart, let alone remember their names.

However, a precocious, energetic and somewhat fussy five-month-old captured our attention and soon became our favourite playmate. Naturally, when Karen spoke to us again the day after our visit, we mentioned Samphauth. Thus, the wheels were set in motion for his adoption.

Becoming A Family

We visited him again in June after learning that we had been given in-principle approval for his adoption. A month later, the final decree was granted by the Cambodian government, which sparked a mad rush for us as we were only given three days' notice to get to Phnom Penh and complete the adoption formalities.

On the morning of 18 July 2008, we flew to Cambodia. That very afternoon, we accepted Samphauth into our care. We then spent another six days in the city, bonding with him and sorting out the remaining red tape so that he could return to Singapore with us.

Looking at the experience through Sam's eyes, we can only imagine what a bewildering experience it must have been for him. In less than a week, he had gone from the quiet rural community, where he had spent the first few months of his life, to the urban bustle of Phnom Penh, before travelling to the strange modern metropolis of Singapore.

Overwhelming as it might have seemed, however, it did not take long for Sam to adapt to his new surroundings in the Lion City. He was readily accepted by our families and close friends, and developed like any ordinary Singaporean toddler would.

Two years after Sam's adoption, we got him a sister. At the time, Cambodia had halted all international adoptions while it reviewed its laws to bring it in line with the Hague Convention*, but we were blessed to be given an opportunity to adopt a three-month-old baby girl from Malaysia. That was how Christina also became a part of our family.

Holding Onto Heritage

Through it all, we never hid from Sam the fact that he had been adopted or that he had been born in Cambodia. We retained his Cambodian name on all of his official documents. We pasted photographs of Kais Village in his life book and watched video clips we had taken of him when he was at the orphanage.

While Sam carried a Singapore passport and pretty much looked and sounded like a typical Singaporean kid, he was also aware of his Cambodian heritage.

As he grew older, he became more and more curious about his home country. We got him a picture book about Cambodia, showed him where it was on a map of the world and read up about the country on the internet.

Sam turned six in 2013. As he was due to enter primary school in the upcoming year, we figured the time was right to make a trip back to Cambodia. So in early November, we returned to Phnom Penh for the first time in five years.

Revisiting Roots

We stayed at the same hotel in Phnom Penh where we had spent our first few days with Sam in 2008. On a Saturday morning, we set out on a 90-kilometre trip to the small village of Treng Trayeoung, where Kais Village orphanage was. The journey took about two and a half hours.

The place had changed since we were last there five years ago. The infant nursery where we had first met Sam still stood, but it had been padlocked and was no longer in use. A similar-looking building that had once housed the toddlers had been demolished following a termite infestation.

In their place nearby stood some larger buildings with red-tiled roofs that housed the kitchen and mess hall, a nursery for the younger kids and a dormitory for the older children who resided there. Brightly lit, spotlessly clean and neatly tiled, with a wide and airy shaded verandah for the children to play on, it was a huge improvement from the dark and fairly rustic building that had once been Sam's home.

As we walked through the compound, we met several children, their local caregivers and a teenage volunteer from Australia who had dedicated a year of her life to teach English to the kids at Kais Village.

One of the English-speaking locals gave us a tour of the new facilities as well as the small farm and orchard where they grew some of the food used to feed the residents of Kais Village.

Sam was initially in a contemplative mood, walking closely by our side and saying little. He did not understand what the other children were saying to him in Khmer, but he gradually warmed to his surroundings. Before long, he was playing and posing for photographs with the kids, including a middle-aged lady who had once been his nanny.

Supporting The Orphanage

It was mid-afternoon when we finally took our leave of Kais Village and headed back to Phnom Penh. Sam did not say much on the journey back to the city. Not surprisingly, he was exhausted and fell asleep in the car.

The directors, Sunny and Karen had been unable to get out to Kompong Speu that day, but we arranged to meet them at our hotel after dinner. Having taken Sam in and naming him six years earlier, Sunny was delighted to see him again.

While Sunny entertained the kids, Karen shared about the challenges they faced in running the orphanage. In the wake of Cambodia's ban on international adoptions, the population of the orphanage had kept growing while a source of revenue to keep the place running had been taken away.

Knowing their plight, we made a monthly contribution in Sam's name for the purchase of rice for Kais Village. It may not have been the biggest of donations, but it was a gesture that was greatly appreciated by Karen and Sunny as they did their best to maintain the community they had taken a decade to build.

Cultural Awareness

We still had a full day in Phnom Penh before our flight back to Singapore, so we took the opportunity to bring Sam and Christina around the city and visit some of its attractions, including the famous Russian Market, Sisowath Quay and the Royal Palace.

The city had undergone much development in the past five years and near the waterfront, where the Tonle Sap River merged with the mighty Mekong, the walkways had been spruced up and several new buildings – including hotels, shopping centres, luxury apartments, offices and even a casino – had popped up.

Yet, for all of the symbols of wealth on display, there were also signs of abject poverty as we saw beggars and street kids desperately trying to make a living for themselves. Having become so accustomed to life in suburban, middle-class Singapore, it was rather shocking for Sam to see firsthand the plight of the underprivileged in Cambodia.

While he is now more Singaporean than Cambodian, Sam still felt connected to the country and he took great pride in the national flag that we had given him. He also asked for a Cambodian map when we passed by a bookshop at the airport.

Feeling Fortunate

I imagine when Sam spoke to Susan on the flight back to Singapore, he probably felt a host of mixed emotions – pleased that he had been able to visit the country of his birth and connect with the place where he had been brought up, yet mindful of how fate had smiled favourably on him.

If he had not been taken in by Kais Village as a newborn, he might not have been given the loving care and attention that he saw the other children receiving there; and if he had not been there on that fateful day of our visit in March five years earlier, we would probably not have met him and made him a part of our family.

However, for Susan and I, we have come to realise that it is not Sam who is the fortunate one, but us. We had been trying unsuccessfully for a number of years to have a child of our own, so when we discovered him at Kais Village, we were overjoyed.

As we watch him grow and develop into a thoughtful, expressive and bright young boy, it only increases our sense that we are truly blessed to have found him.

For Sam, the matter of why we had chosen him may have been important. But for us, what mattered was the fact that we had become a family.

Sam is now our son. Whether he identifies more with Singapore or Cambodia, he is, in every way, our very own.

* The Hague Convention on the Protection of Children and Co-operation in Respect of Inter-Country Adoption (Hague Adoption Convention) is an international agreement to establish safeguards to ensure that inter-country adoptions take place in the best interests of the child. Cambodia ratified the Convention in 2007 and suspended all international adoptions in December 2009 due to concerns over child trafficking.

This is the sequel to the story "Finding Sam" first published in Our Very Own (2010).

8

What If

Alice

"As adoptive parents, we will do our best to prepare her for the future, but we will not be able to prepare the future for her."

This is something I think about constantly, as do many adoptive parents.

What if my child's birth parents want to meet her when she grows up?

What if she wants to meet them?

What if she doesn't?

Initially I did not think about it much when our daughter first came home with us at less than a month old. The frustrations of trying to conceive a biological child quickly faded away as Mun Tarng (whose name means "the family is complete" in Mandarin) captured our hearts in October 2007. My husband and I had travelled to Malaysia to meet her birth mother and promised we would take care of her baby as our forever family.

After many years of soul-searching and watching others interact with adopted children, we were finally ready to be adoptive parents. Fortunately, we have several adoptees in our network of family and friends, so it was natural for them to welcome our daughter.

Other adoptive parents shared that they had benefited from being able to keep in contact with the birth parents, as it provided an identity and a history for their adopted child. Friends and relatives who were adoptees also shared similar thoughts on how they finally connected with their birth parents and biological siblings.

Finding The Birth Parents

The search for birth parents is not always easy. In our daughter's first year with us, we decided to search for her birth parents.

We went through several sources but were told it was not possible to locate them. After two years, we tried again – this time on our own – only to find out that the birth parents were actually still living at the same address listed on the copy of the identity cards that had been given to us!

We drove to their home in Malaysia and rang the bell at the gate, completely unannounced. Her birth father came out to meet us. We recognised him right away from his photo in the adoption documents.

We explained the reason why we wanted to stay in touch with them. We showed him pictures of Mun Tarng and thanked him for the lovely daughter who has brought so much joy to our family.

We asked if they would like to meet with Mun Tarng. The birth father said he would have to discuss it with his wife, who was not home at the time. We left our contact numbers, hoping they would get in touch with us. We waited and waited, but did not hear from them.

Trying Again

Another year passed by. With encouragement from my husband, we decided to make another attempt the following year. We drove to Malaysia again during the Chinese New Year period.

Like the last visit, we showed up unannounced. This time, we got to meet with her birth mother.

We were invited into the house, where we also met Mun Tarng's three biological siblings. We chatted for about 20 minutes and exchanged phone numbers and email addresses. I told the birth mother to just call me whenever she was ready to meet Mun Tarng.

It remains at the back of my mind that someday I may get "that call". I wonder if my daughter will be ready.

Knowing Her Story

I started telling Mun Tarng about her adoption story when she was a few months old. She knows she has birth parents who live in Malaysia and that she has siblings.

As it often happens, adoptive parents might think that their children are not thinking about it, as they seem so matter-of-fact or dismissive when told the facts. They do not yet express much emotion about it.

One day, out of the blue, while we were on a trip to Malaysia, Mun Tarng suddenly asked:

"Are we going to meet my tummy mummy?"

"No, not this time," we told her.

She accepted the answer without question, but she remembered.

When Mun Tarng was five years old, we were having dinner one day at a hawker centre with some friends and we were talking about siblings. Totally unprompted, Mun Tarng reported to the others that she has two brothers and one sister (even though she is an only child in our family!) in Malaysia.

She had definitely internalised what we had been sharing with her.

It Is Her Choice

I have thought through all this very carefully. I have started making a memory box for her and I am thinking about what I will say in the event that she asks "Why me?".

I have decided that if her birth parents say they want to meet and if Mun Tarng is ready, I will likely tell her more of the details about her adoption. If either her birth parents or Mun Tarng decide they are not ready, I may keep the story simple, so as to spare her some of the details.

I believe that it is the birth parents and the child who should decide when the time is right to meet, not the adoptive parents. But deep in my heart, I keep hoping that it will happen sometime in the near future.

The important thing is, *everyone* in the equation has to be ready. As adoptive parents, we will do our best to prepare her for the future, but we will not be able to prepare the future for her.

What if they want to?

What if they don't?

These questions will always be on my mind.

This is the sequel to the story "Our Child Finally Arrives" first published in Our Very Own (2010).

9

Adopting No. 2

Low Bee Lian

"Adoption: Our family is like a big patchwork quilt. Each of us different yet stitched together by love."

- Unknown

I t all started in 2010 when Caleb turned two years old. In a blink of an eye, we had celebrated his second birthday.

I was sure I wanted to adopt another baby. Why not? This time, I wanted to be more involved in looking after the baby. Caleb only came to Singapore when he was four months old, so I missed out on his early months, save for a week when I was alone with him in a hotel in Thailand.

So, in March 2010, we began our second Home Study Report application, and with the Home Visit done in July, the paperwork was completed on 13 September 2010.

Initially, I was convinced I wanted a girl to complete my family. During the process, however, I became open to having another boy again. After all, it was more important to let Caleb have a sibling whom he could grow up together with. What did it matter which gender the sibling was?

Moreover, my silly spouse jokingly remarked that if we had a girl who grew up alongside a handsome brother, what if a romantic situation developed? You know, like in those Korean drama soap operas where A loves B who loves C, and where the female sibling could have harboured love towards the brother.

It could happen in real life too, right? After all, don't all TV dramas draw their inspirations from real life? Of course, I would not like it happening under my roof!

Bringing Baby Home

It was a Tuesday afternoon on 14 September 2010, after a happy lunch gathering with my friends. I was on my way to fetch Caleb from my mother's house when the phone call came. It was Teo Seok Bee from TOUCH Adoption Services, informing me that a two-week-old baby boy was available for adoption.

"Local babies are hard to come by," I was told. There is a supposedly long queue.

"Why me?" I wondered.

I had never expected that I would be in line for a local baby and was all prepared to accept a foreign baby. I had even liaised with an adoption agency already. (Once the Home Study Report was obtained, I was ready to meet any suitable baby at the adoption agency.)

This particular baby boy was born at KK Women's and Children's Hospital. After he was discharged, a difficult decision was made by his family to place him in foster care for a week while waiting for adoption. I heard that his initial adoption fell through and, by God's grace, my wait for a second child was short.

Two days later, on an auspicious Thursday afternoon, together with my mother-in-law and Caleb, we brought Caden home.

Adjusting To Two

Caden had a very different temperament compared to Caleb, who was a really easy baby. Caleb smiled a lot and was easy to please. He also fed well and slept without fuss… while Caden really stretched me.

My second son needed more carrying, more cuddling and more pacifying while I needed more patience and more sleep. There were nights when his frequent waking and fussing exhausted me. I thought that period would never end. His whining and wailing were so constant that I almost became depressed.

Miraculously, at about six months, Caden began to look very cute – and has grown cuter day by day. He made me laugh at his silly expressions and the things he did.

However, sibling squabbling became a constant feature! Every five minutes, I found myself either shouting at Caleb to stop teasing Caden or telling Caden to stop crying.

Somehow, through the constant teasing (by Caleb, the cheeky one), their brotherly bond began to grow. Even though outwardly, strangers may say they do not look like brothers, but to them, they *are* brothers – and that is enough for them and me.

Family Identity

With that, my family is complete. Like Caleb, I have retained many keepsakes for Caden – his green nappy wrap and the outfit that he came home in, the letter from the foster mother who took care of him for a week and his love gift from the birth family.

Often, when I am out with my boys, I get lots of questions from complete strangers:

"Is your husband an Indian/Malay?"

"Your elder boy looks like a Malay, but the young one looks like you!"

"Your boys so handsome!" or "Are they brothers? How come they look so different?"

I always give affirmative answers: "Yes they are! They are my sons!"

With no further need to elaborate, I just smile and briskly walk off.

Caleb has been told that he was born in Thailand and came to live in Singapore when he was five months old. He has a Thailand mommy and he lives with the Singapore mommy. He has his Singapore father and his Heavenly Father.

When Caleb was a year old, we made a trip to Thailand. Incidentally, it was the season of Songkran celebrating the traditional Thai New Year. At this festival, Caleb had a taste of the showers of blessings.

His birth mother spent a few days with us. She has since gone on to complete her university studies in Bangkok, and can speak and write English. Our efforts to acquaint Caleb with the Thai language have been limited by our limited knowledge of it. Perhaps we might send him to learn Thai if he wishes to pick it up in the future.

Best Brothers

With my husband's overseas work posting currently, he is away most months. At the moment, it is just me and my boys, and my in-laws lend a hand.

Most days, I bring them with me wherever I go, be it to the library, my parents' house, church or to run errands.

The boys miss their father very much. Whenever my husband is back, we would go out and play. We even took two weeks' vacation to Bali and Cambodia, just to build travel memories and bond as a family.

Other than that, our usual routine involves attending school and then going for piano or swimming lessons. Caleb will be starting primary school next year, so that will be another exciting stage to look forward to.

Being a book lover myself, I am glad I was able to influence them to like books from young. By frequently reading to them, and with some help in phonics training, Caleb was able to read rather fluently in kindergarten. Hopefully, he can do the same in Chinese too.

The boys are also able to sit still and read by themselves, while I catch up with housework or take some time for myself. They also enjoy constructing creative models using LEGO or enact their own stories when they play together. Children can be so imaginative!

"Mummy, we are best brothers!" Sometimes the boys tell me that, which amuses me.

Despite all the constant bickering, whining and tantrums, I am always thankful that God has been so gracious to bless me with two beautiful angels.

This is the sequel to the story "Finally Home" first published in Our Very Own (2010).

10

Nursing The Adoption Wound

Andrea Yee

"I love all my two mommies and two daddies.
My heart is big enough for all of you!"

After struggling with infertility for five years, we now have two beautiful girls who became a part of our family through adoption. Jane is 10 years old today and Lisa just turned five. Both of them have a close and beautiful sibling relationship which we are in awe of whenever we witness those moments of grace.

When Lisa was three, something transpired in her understanding. We were walking from her classroom to our car when we had this conversation.

Lisa: Mommy, my best friend Emily said she has only one mommy and one daddy. Why does Emily have only one mommy but I have two?

Me: That is because her mommy and daddy are together. Remember, I told you that your tummy mummy and tummy daddy are not together, that is why they cannot bring you up and they found us to be your forever mommy and forever daddy.

Lisa: Why can't my tummy mummy look after me?

Me: It is hard to bring up a baby on her own. She needs to work to buy milk powder, diapers and send you to school. If she does not go to work, she won't have the money to do all that for you.

Lisa: So… if you have no money, you cannot have a baby?

Me: *(My mind went into a slight shock, wondering how to disassociate in her young mind between having money and having a baby. No! I had to change this association!)* No, baby, I meant that she would not be able to go to work and look after you at the same time.

Lisa: But my tummy daddy can look after me…

Me: My darling, they were not staying together. That is why he cannot look after you too.

(I thought this explanation would suffice, but her unexpected response broke my heart.)

Lisa: *(bowing her head and said dejectedly)* That means they both don't (sic) want me.

Me: *(Jumping into rescue mode and trying my best to choke back tears)* My darling, they both knew they were unable to look after you because they were not together. That is why they asked Aunty Seok Bee and Aunty Wei Lei to find mommy, daddy and Jie Jie (big sister) to be your family and look after you. We love you soooo soooo much. And there is Gong Gong, Mama, Grandpa too…

I went on to list our immediate family members who love her a lot and then quickly texted my hubby to tell him about this conversation.

He, too, was heartbroken. Immediately we set up a "conference call" in the car where my husband continued assuring Lisa about how much she is wanted by us and how grateful we were to her birth parents for giving us the chance to be her forever parents.

She did not seem upset throughout the "conference call", but we knew that she had come to a realisation then – that is, in order to be in our family, she had to be unwanted by her first set of parents.

This is the harsh reality which all adopted children have to go through. I was just unprepared for it to dawn on her so soon.

Assurance Of Love

A week after that conversation with Lisa, she was asked to do a family tree at school. I made it a point to add "tummy mummy" and "tummy daddy" on the page. I also checked in with her form teacher, Ms Toni, to find out if she had ever mentioned anything about her tummy mummy or tummy daddy. At that point, apparently she had not.

Two months later, Ms Toni filled me in on a conversation Lisa had with her on the bus during a class excursion.

Lisa: Ms Toni, you know, I have two mommies and two daddies. My tummy mummy and daddy knew they could not look after me, so they chose my mommy and daddy to take me as their daughter and look after me.

Ms Toni: Wow! And I know they both love you very much. Thank you for sharing this with me.

Bedtime is the period when our kids are most open to chatting and processing issues which had happened during the day. That night, I decided to take the opportunity to "throw a pebble" and see what kind of "ripples" I would get from the questions I posed.

I must admit, I was still rather rattled by the conversation we had had two months ago. I was worried that Lisa was still feeling unwanted and wondered if anything had changed. If it did, was it for the better or for worse?

Me: Ms Toni told me you shared with her that you have two mommies and two daddies…

Lisa: Yes.

Me: What did you tell her?

Lisa: *(looking at me with big doleful eyes)* I told her my tummy mummy and daddy asked you and daddy to love me.

Me: Yes! Yes! And you know we do! *(I scooped her up in my arms and we did a happy dance.)*

A month later, again at bedtime, Lisa asked:

Lisa: Mommy, do you have a photo of my tummy mummy?

Me: Hmmm, let me check if I have one. Why do you ask?

Lisa: She's my mommy and I love her.

Me: You know what, I love her too because she gave us the chance to be YOUR mommy and daddy!

Lisa: Do you have a photo of my daddy?

Me: That one I might not have. Why?

Lisa: Because I love him too. I love all my two mommies and two daddies. My heart is big enough for all of you! Plus, Jie Jie, Gong Gong, Mama, Grandpa….

Within a period of three months, it dawned on me that Lisa had gone through an entire thought process. *She had had an epiphany about being adopted!*

Although I totally support and understand the importance of disclosure, I often thought of it as reopening the primal wound of rejection and unwantedness which I so badly wanted to be healed as early as possible. As her mom, I instinctively wanted to prevent this wound from hurting her. Why reopen a wound that has closed and supposedly healed?

The moment Lisa realised what being adopted meant, figuratively speaking, it seemed like her old wound had been sliced open and she was feeling the pain and bleeding all over again.

It was something so hard for me to witness as a grown-up. When I knew I could not stem this wound, I surrendered her to God and trusted Him to sort it out in her heart and her head.

As much as I did not want to have that wound reopened, I now realise it was a necessary step towards real healing. When Lisa and I had those series of chats, we had reopened it tenderly with love, nursing it with explanations and gentle truth in order for the wound to heal beautifully instead of merely allowing it to close without dealing with its roots.

I may never know the depth of this primal wound. When will it open and bleed again? Are there other wounds still yet to be discovered?

I may not be the one to nurse it all or be there when it happens. All I know is that I want to be there for my daughters when they have to deal with it whenever issues arise, even if it means simply holding them whilst the wounds get tended to.

I want to remind them that they are loved oh-so-much. I want to cry with them and celebrate with them too. To me, this is the essence of how an adoptive family seals its bond as a family that is built on love and trust – by being there for each other, through thick or thin.

This is the sequel to the story "Becoming A Family" first published in Our Very Own (2010).

PART 3

ADOPTING FROM OVERSEAS

11

Growing Our Family

Ernest Lee and Jin Wang

"Adoption is not just a matter between my wife and I. It also concerns our extended families and even the community around us."

The option of adoption is probably not the first thing on the minds of married couples – at least not for my wife Jin and I, although we did discuss it briefly before we got married. When the time came to start a family, we were, like most couples, trying to conceive biological children.

My wife and I had agreed not to have children for the first two years of our marriage. However, when we felt we were ready, the wait seemed to take forever. We consulted doctors and followed their advice to measure temperatures and chart graphs, but had no success month after month.

At the same time, our parents kept asking us when we were going to have a baby, so you can imagine the pressure and frustrations we faced back then.

Most of our church friends were praying for us while we kept trying. Sometime in 1997/1998, a director who was running two foreign orphanages came to speak at our church. His dream was to help every orphan find a family and he said that *God made families, not institutions, to look after children.*

It struck me that there were many children without families and yet there we were, trying to conceive. We were already open to the idea of adoption and felt the conviction to adopt at that church service. So my wife and I decided to start our adoption journey.

Surprise!

To get going, we had all the supporting letters from our doctor, employer and pastor prepared. But just when we were about to mail the application package to the relevant authorities, my wife conceived!

It was a welcome surprise and everyone was very excited. The adoption plan was naturally shelved. It was a tough pregnancy, but after being in and out of hospital seven times, my wife gave birth to our son in 1999.

It was during our family's annual thanksgiving cum planning session at the end of 1999 when my wife and I discussed plans for another child. Both of us felt we had some unfinished business and that we had already become adoptive parents spiritually. So we mailed the package that we had prepared earlier and started looking for an adoption agency to help us.

Adoption is not just a matter between my wife and I. It also concerns our extended families and even the community around us.

We shared our plans with our parents – and just as we had expected, they raised many questions like, "You are still young and can still try to conceive" or "Why adopt?" or "What if the baby is unhealthy?" etc.

In short, they were against it. We assured them that adopting did not mean we would stop trying to conceive. In the end, they knew we had already made up our minds.

Connecting The Dots

My wife and I were quite particular about adopting from an orphanage, to be certain of the child's status as an orphan.

The search for our "treasure" brought us to Vietnam. After an unpleasant experience with the adoption agency, our church friend Violet said she could introduce us to a Vietnamese friend who might be able to help.

In 2000, we flew to Vietnam with our son and Violet, where she introduced us to Mr Long. Mr Long had never been involved in any adoption process before, but he was very willing to help us because he considered it a noble deed.

On my second visit to Vietnam, Mr Long brought me to visit the orphanage and make initial inquiries. Every cot in the baby room was occupied. Knowing the babies were all orphans needing a home somehow made the room feel rather cold. It was unlike the cosy nurseries in the delivery wards back in Singapore, where the babies had families waiting for them.

Our Chosen One

The orphanage's policy did not allow us to choose the baby we wanted to adopt. I could only tell them our preferred age range and gender. Not long after, I was surprised to receive photographs of two babies, both only two months old. Mr Long told me that he would try to select Baby A for us.

From the two photos, I was actually more drawn to Baby B, who showed a determined face with a clenched fist. Somehow, I felt a certain connection with her, even though Baby A looked cuter. Since I was not able to see the babies personally, I kept my thoughts to myself. I simply told Mr Long that the baby should preferably be active and healthy and left the arrangements to him.

A few days later, Mr Long informed us that Baby B would be matched to us because she was the more active one. I was so pleased that Baby B was the chosen one! Shortly after, Mr Long helped to arrange for Baby B to be taken care of by a nanny outside the orphanage.

Our Expanding Family

Since she was going to be ours, we started picking a name for her. In Chinese, "宁" (pronounced "ning") means peace and we chose it because it was our hope that she would always find peace in God. To help her retain her Vietnamese roots, we spelt it "Ninh", in order to retain the characteristic "nh" seen in many Vietnamese words.

Would you believe though, two weeks after I told Mr Long to proceed with the adoption of Ninh, my wife conceived again! My wife and I knew that there was no turning back.

We wanted both babies – the one from the orphanage and the one in the womb. Both were ours.

Some weeks later, I received a calendar with Ninh's A5-sized photo. Oddly, either the photo was taken from a wrong angle or she really looked like a boy. To be honest, I could not say the baby in the photo looked pretty. But since she was ours now, it did not matter. We knew we would love her just the same.

I hung the photo calendar on the wall so that we could see her every day. The wait for the procedures to be completed seemed to take ages. Perhaps the wait was necessary for us to develop an attachment and love for the baby over time.

As my wife had early contractions, she could not travel to Vietnam to see Ninh. So I travelled on my own, staying just a day or two, to visit our little baby and settle the administrative work. As always, Mr Long was a good host and I am ever so grateful to him for his assistance throughout this process.

Ninh's birth mother had delivered her in a hospital and left quietly the next day. While in Vietnam, I asked Mr Long if I could place an advertisement to get her birth parents to contact me.

Although I had not thought about what I would do after knowing who the birth parents were, I just felt that it was something I had to do for Ninh, should she ask about it when she grows up. However, I was advised that many would respond to the advertisement and I would have a hard time identifying the real birth parents. So I had no choice but to abandon the idea.

More Than One Homecoming

After a few months of administrative procedures, the day finally came for me to bring Ninh back to Singapore! My mother went to Vietnam with me and we brought Ninh back on our first son's second birthday. Everyone was very excited and we had a good celebration.

By then, our son Angus was sleeping in his own room and Ninh took over his cot in our room. Our son was a good older brother. Both of them got along well and enjoyed playing together.

An adoptive mother's love is no less than the love for her baby in the womb. I witnessed this on several occasions when my wife would cry because she wanted to be a better mother to Ninh. However, due to the early contractions with her pregnancy and medication she was on, she was not able to carry Ninh as much as she would like.

Four months after Ninh arrived, our second son Amos was born. We had an even more challenging time when somehow, my wife ended up with numbness on her left leg and foot-drop (difficulty in lifting her foot). She left the hospital in a wheelchair. Thankfully, after going through therapy and acupuncture, she recovered completely within six months.

There were moments when we were really torn between having to care for our newborn and Ninh at the same time. At times, it felt a little strange too – after all, we were adoptive parents for the first time and we had not yet had the opportunity to learn from other adoptive parents. We simply had to jump straight into the deep end.

My wife was a part-time music teacher, so her working hours were more flexible. After our domestic helper completed her contract, we did not hire a new one. The children were between one and three years old then. I think we managed our parents' expectations quite well and there were no subsequent murmurs from any of them about the adoption. After all, as a Chinese family, we already had two boys, so what could anyone say?

We were still open to have another child, but we felt that it would be best if it were not to be a girl so that there would not be any chance for anyone, especially the grandparents, to compare Ninh with her sister. However, I was really curious to know how our birth daughter would look like since our biological sons look alike.

About a year later, my wife conceived the third time! This must be due to all the prayers our friends had been saying on our behalf! We had to tell our friends to stop praying for us to have more children after that!

I think God knew our concerns about comparisons and did not want us to worry too much, so guess what? He gave us another boy.

A Mother's EDD

In 2012, we joined TOUCH Adoptive Families Network (TAFNET) to connect with this special community and learn from fellow adoptive families. At one of the TAFNET home group meetings, some adoptive mothers shared that they did not have an EDD (Estimated Date of Delivery).

I corrected them and told them we most certainly did – we had *Estimated Disclosure Date!*

My wife and I had agreed that we should let Ninh know about her background and to do it early. *There is nothing wrong with adoption and there is absolutely nothing to hide.* There was no other way for us to explain why her birth certificate listed Vietnam as her birth place, and not Singapore. In our case, we also had to prepare our boys for the truth.

Ever since our children were toddlers, we had a routine of telling them bedtime stories. Many of the stories would have a message on moral values. So one day, we tested the waters by telling them a story about how a poor couple reluctantly left their baby at the orphanage because they could not afford to bring their baby up. The baby was then adopted by a couple who had another child at home.

We then asked them what they felt about what the birth parents did, what the adoptive parents did, how they would feel if they were in the shoes of the adopted child and then in the place of the biological child in the family. Thank God their responses were all positive!

When the children were younger, our frequent getaway was Genting Highlands in Malaysia. To go anywhere further would have cost a bomb! On one of our trips, we disclosed to the children over lunch:

"Ninh, you remember the story we told about the baby that was adopted? Actually, you are like the baby. You were also adopted. Daddy and Mommy love you very much."

Ninh was only three and a half years old then. She just acknowledged what I said and did not say anything else as she was probably more interested in her lunch and the rides at theme park she would take after that.

The boys did not say anything either. Did we choose the right place and time for the disclosure? I do not know. But what I do know is, having made the disclosure, we felt a burden lifted from our hearts. We would have to continue to manage and respond as we go along.

Factual Reckoning

When Ninh was eight years old, in Primary Two, my wife received a call from her form teacher. The teacher wanted to confirm if Ninh was adopted. Apparently, Ninh had "announced" it to her teacher and some friends in class, probably because they were discussing something related to adoption, children or orphanage.

Two years later, while I was looking for something in the cabinet, Ninh was beside me and I showed her the file with all her adoption papers (several had to be translated to English, of course).

It was totally unplanned. As I flipped through the pages with her, I was quite nervous, wondering how she might react, what she would say and what questions she would ask. But she simply inquired about basic information and walked off.

Ninh was about 10 years old then. Since then, she has asked to see the documents only once. We have plans to bring our whole family to visit Vietnam next year (2016).

I used to consider birthdays as an opportunity for the birthday child to simply have a good time. But since I became a father myself, I have come to realise that the birthday of the adopted child is also a significant day for the birth parents.

I could not help but wonder how Ninh's birth mother might have felt after giving birth to her. I believe she had decided not to take the path of least resistance – that is, to opt for an abortion. It was her intention all along to leave the hospital quietly after giving birth.

On Ninh's 14th birthday, I felt the urge to honour her birth mother when I had a quiet time with Ninh. I reminded Ninh that it must have been a very difficult decision for her birth mother and she must also be thinking about her little girl on this special day.

For the first time, we prayed together for God to bless her birth mother wherever she may be.

Propelled By Love

Whether their children are adopted or not, every family goes through ups and downs. Ours is no different. In the course of sibling squabbles, Ninh has heard her younger brothers say, "You were not born by mommy!".

Needless to say, we addressed the negative behaviour immediately. Thankfully, it has happened less than 10 times, although Ninh thinks it is more than that. Although we have disclosed her adoption to her, we would not take things for granted and assume that things will be fine.

We are still part of a TAFNET home group and lately, I have been pondering how to respond if I were to hear Ninh say:

"Don't tell me what to do! I don't need you! You are not my real daddy!"

I hope that day will never come. But if it does come, my response will be: "You may not see me as your real daddy, but you are my real daughter! That will never change."

Ninh has been our daughter for almost 15 years now. There are still times when I reflect and wonder how we managed to take that first step and bring her home all the way from Vietnam.

Looking back, I know it was God's love that propelled us. We hope our children would be open to following our footsteps to be a loving family to other children in need.

May God continue to give us the wisdom and grace we all need, both now and in the future.

12

The Light At The End Of
The Tunnel Is Love

Soo Sing

"You were there when no one else was.
You wanted me when no one else did.
You loved me when no one else did.
Love you, mom and dad."

Parenting is tough. Don't get me wrong. There are many good days but there are also rough days.

I remember the early days, having to carry my daughter to sleep through the night. I was not surviving too well, with only two to three hours' sleep for months on end.

I remember going for holidays where there was no fan or air-conditioning and my son cried through the night. I had to walk/carry him on the beach to calm him.

I remember the long flight to Europe, our first long-distance trip with a young child. He could not sleep on the seat, but was too big to be in a bassinet. We snuck him onto the floor, where he slept until the stewardess came and woke him up because he was not supposed to sleep there. It was a loonnnggg whiny/crying night. I swore that was going to be the last trip we would take!

There were days of struggling with school and homework, or awaiting the dreaded calls from the school. How in the world do our kids manage to find new ways of getting into trouble? It just seemed to get worse, year after year.

I remember the days of missing children, disappearing after school without a word. We hunted high and low everywhere, knocking on friends' doors and searching every inch of the school to find one little child who decided to wander off without telling us.

I remember the trips to hospitals – in wild panic – with a sick child.

I remember the time I brought my disobedient hysterical son to the toilet. He was screaming at the top of his lungs in the toilet cubicle. Then all of a sudden, I heard a knock on the door by a stranger, asking me to stop hitting my child – except I had not even started yet!

I see the light at the end of the tunnel, only to find an oncoming train.

Fifteen years on, it took a painful separation of just two months – when he left for studies in Australia – for my son to post this:

"You were there when no one else was.
You wanted me when no one else did.
You loved me when no one else did.

Love you, mom and dad."

His post blew me away. I was speechless – which is rare.

I gasp, gather my thoughts, memories racing through my mind before, finally... finally, I see a light at the end of the tunnel.

This time, it truly is a silver lining – the light at the end of a long tunnel, which makes it all worthwhile. The light that is... love.

My heart melts as I realise, yes, it is all worth it.

That painful separation had somehow given the clarity of unclouded love. I saw my son as never before – a young, mature (mostly) boy all grown up, almost at the edge of manhood.

To my son:

"Yes, son, we made the choice to love you 15 years ago. Love endures the ups and downs. Kind of like how God loves us. It was the right decision.

Thank you for giving us a chance and forgiving our mistakes, of which there are many.

We love you then and we love you now – we will always love you.

Love, Dad."

13

I Choose to Love Her

The Vass Family

*"I did not fall in love with this child – **I** chose to love her. It is about commitment and love – and this, we will provide."*

From excitement to shock, from happiness to guilt and frustration, from anger to thankfulness and love… These are the tumultuous feelings I (Veronica) have had – and still have – since we adopted Madeline about 10 months ago. These emotions have caused me to feel and act in ways I never knew I was capable of.

When my husband Steve and I got married in 2001, we started trying for a family right away but nothing happened. Through medical help, I became pregnant in 2004. Unfortunately, due to some pregnancy complications, my biological daughter Bernadette was born premature at six months gestational age and passed away shortly thereafter in 2005.

At that point, we thought that God wanted us to share and give our love to another child who needed it instead of us having our "own". That was when we started our application to adopt.

A Waiting Game

The wait to be matched with a child from China was supposed to be 12 months from the time of application, but then it got stretched to three years, then to five years, then indefinitely.

During this waiting time, we were "offered" three local newborn babies but for various reasons, they all did not work out. It was an emotional rollercoaster, but we always trusted that God had His plans and would provide in His time.

While the wait continued (the truth is, we were losing hope that it was ever going to happen), I became pregnant again in 2006. Unfortunately, this pregnancy also ended in a miscarriage. Needless to say, it was a tough period where we relied on our love and faith to carry us through.

The following year, we were blessed with a biological child. Our first son Gregory was born in 2007 and he quickly became a focal point in our lives.

We wanted more children and the joy of having Gregory only fueled our resolve to continue to grow our family. In 2010, by God's grace, we were blessed with our second son Christopher.

Throughout the delivery of our sons, we continued to update our home study and remained current with our application. The last opportunity to adopt was while I was pregnant with Christopher. We were hopeful in that calling, but when it did not happen, we felt that our chances for adoption had run their due course. After all, we had already missed out on multiple adoptions over several years.

Unexpected Development

Then in September 2013, out of the blue, we received a call from TOUCH Adoption Services, informing us that that we had been matched with a two-year-old girl in China.

A month or two ago, my husband and I had just been wondering if we were even on any lists anymore. It had been so long since we last checked on our application status! After eight years of waiting, a child was waiting for us!

I could not imagine how drastically our family dynamics would change. The decision we were about to make would not only affect our lives, but also the lives of our two boys who were six and three years old respectively at the time.

Our hearts immediately said "yes", but we took one day to just talk between us, husband and wife. Then we spent the rest of the week involving the boys in the discussion.

We asked them how they felt and played devil's advocate, telling them about what it means to be the big brothers who would have to give in and share. They would have to grow up and let the little sister be the baby of the family.

Interestingly, they both agreed enthusiastically and did not waver at all throughout the week. The boys were as much a part of this as we were, so we wanted to make sure we included them in the decision-making process.

Finally, as a family, we decided to proceed with the adoption and love this girl for the rest of our lives. It was like committing to a relationship with someone even before we went on a blind date with them!

All four of us travelled to China together, and on 28 October 2013, we met our little girl Madeline and became a family of five.

The Orphanage Effect

When the nanny brought Madeline to meet us, she did not cry nor turn back even once to look for her nanny. She was focused on us and made *us* feel wanted! It was as if she had been ready for this to happen.

She played well with her brothers and expressed interest in everything we said to her. She laughed when we played with her. Although she did not speak at all, she could understand when we spoke to her in Mandarin. We all seemed to like each other, extending every consideration as if we knew we would all have to be understanding in the transition.

Our hearts broke for the first time for her when she accidentally knocked her head (hard) at the corner of the hotel room desk. Yet she did not cry at all! She only cringed and quietly rubbed her head, then moved on.

That is when the reality of her life in an orphanage dawned on us – that she was just one of the many children there and no one had time to focus on the little falls the children had.

When we hugged and kissed her, there was no response whatsoever. She looked at us as if to say, "What are you guys doing?" It was as if she had never experienced love through the expressions of hugs and kisses before.

It made me feel rather sad. Emotionally, she was an island unto herself and we began to see this more and more in her behaviour.

What we did not expect was when we first tried to give her a shower back at the hotel. She would scream and pull away from us as soon as the tap was turned on, pushing herself into a corner of the bathroom, squatting down while covering her face to block us out and screaming at the top of her lungs.

It was a traumatic experience for us. We could not understand why she reacted this way, except to surmise that perhaps she had had a bad experience before.

For the next two weeks in China, each time before shower time, Steve and I had to prepare ourselves mentally and be ready physically to struggle with Madeline.

Things got better after one week, but we still had to be extremely calm and careful before each shower time. (I am pleased to report that within a year after she joined our family, she became confident in the water and started swimming like a fish! Indeed, we have come a long way.)

Fitting In At Home

When we brought Madeline back to Singapore, everything was new to her – from the country, the people, new foods, strange smells and foreign languages to our home, her bed and new toys, among myriad other things.

Outwardly, our little Madeline seemed to be adapting very well. She participated in all our family activities and interactions positively. The only sign we received that demonstrated her stress with this new life was when she woke up in the middle of the night screaming and crying. This went on for two months.

We let her sleep in our bed with us for six months as we wanted her to feel secure and loved. Besides the crying in the middle of the night, we also noticed that she would not let us hug her to sleep initially. She pushed us away as she fell asleep – obviously she was not used to being cuddled. She only learnt to cuddle up to sleep after a couple of weeks.

We could sense that she was also struggling to adjust to her new environment. She was trying very hard to adapt, but we could see that she was also frustrated and often resorted to behaviours that had worked for her at the orphanage – namely, throwing tantrums and showing aggressiveness.

Both our boys were adapting to their roles as big brothers. They were being very understanding and willing to share. Even Christopher who was the "baby" was so pleased to be the "little big brother" and was keen to share with his new sister. So when Madeline reverted to her survival mode, being sharp and self-serving, it was tough for the boys who were really being accommodating and trying their best to help her to adapt.

As "new parents" in this relationship, we had invested so much emotionally, leaving ourselves vulnerable to heartache, but we were prepared and accepted that the process of adjustment would take time.

So we persevered, trying to provide a loving, secure and stable environment where she would be comfortable and start to open up. There was never any doubt that we were committed to working it out, but the challenges were so new and foreign to us that we had to learn to adapt quickly.

Fitting In At School

Before we met Madeline, we thought it would be a good idea not to send her to school for at least six months to a year. We thought that if she could spend that time with us, it would help to reinforce the message that we were going to be her forever mommy and daddy.

However, after observing her challenges a few weeks after her arrival, we changed our minds.

What was concerning was that, at two years old, she was not uttering a single word that we could understand. It was not the language; she was just not uttering any words at all. She could understand most of what we said to her, but she could not "talk", which contributed to a lot of frustration for her as well as us, since there was a communication breakdown in more ways than one!

We figured she might have been under-stimulated at the orphanage and thought that perhaps a more constructive and structured environment would help her. She expressed curiosity and seemed keen to learn and understand. We needed to expose her to English and Mandarin languages, so we could all communicate better. Hence, we sent her to a childcare with our middle child, Christopher.

The first few months were rough for the teachers too. Madeline threw tantrums at school and we would often hear from Christopher and his classmates about how Madeline "screams and cries so much"!

We could only imagine how tough it must have been for the teachers as they did not have the ability to discipline as we did as parents. We were honest with them about her background and what we identified as challenges, sharing our frustrations and successes while collaborating with them to make it work.

Thankfully, over the next six months, Madeline went from being the child whom teachers did not want to deal with, to the child everyone wanted to adopt after seeing her transformation! The frustrated child who once threw herself onto the floor kicking and screaming was now a bright and engaging girl who sang along and enthusiastically participated in class.

Evidently, the structure and stimulation was the right choice. All this was made possible only with the help and careful coordination with the teachers at the school. Without their understanding and buy-in, it might not have worked at all.

Their love and creativity, particularly her direct teacher Miss Fu Yao Mei, was a big part of the success we now enjoy. Madeline loved it there and she became well-loved by the teachers as well. Seeing how she had blossomed, we were affirmed that this was one of the best decisions we had made.

Retraining Responses

Madeline's survival instincts were very strong. Having grown up in the orphanage since she was only two to three months old, Madeline had to rely on herself on many fronts. She is still very possessive over her things and when she wants something, she wants it her way and in her time.

Before, when she did not get what she wanted, she would throw herself on the floor, scream and cry at the top of her lungs. When it first happened, we accepted it as part of the transitional period. However, after a few weeks of multiple times sprawling on the floor daily, I was exasperated! I never had to deal with such behaviour with my two sons.

Steve and I had to decide if this was a habit or a personality issue; or was it just survival instincts; or was it her "terrible twos" kicking in... ?

We had no answers! However, what we did agree on was this was just not an acceptable behaviour in our family and we needed to convey this message clearly to her. She was our daughter and it was our job to correct the behaviour constructively.

To do this, we needed to decide on a disciplinary method that was firm, yet without causing trauma to her. We gave her "Time In" by making her sit on a sofa in our living room each time she threw herself on the floor (this sofa became a big part of her daily routine for the next three months).

In the beginning, she would struggle terribly. We had to physically pin her against the sofa. Lots of struggling, lots of screaming and lots of crying... it was tough!

After three months, Madeline finally began to learn that tantrums were not the way to achieve her objectives and the tantrums eventually subsided. (Thank God!)

Committed To A Choice

Madeline has a very strong personality and she does not give in easily. It was challenging to get her to cooperate in the beginning. She would fight to get her way all the time.

We do not want to change who she is; we want to help her become the best person she can be – but she was not making it easy for us to do so!

As I battled my own exasperation, I struggled with my feelings. Doubt crept in and I questioned if I was really capable of loving a non-biological child, and if I was going to be able to handle the transition. My husband even remarked that he wondered if I was committed to the adoption, given how I was reacting in the process of coming to terms with my own emotions.

After talking to my friends (and talking a lot to myself!) as well as praying about it, I finally came to a conclusion: I did not fall in love with this child – I *chose* to love her.

This is going to be a journey of love – and it might be a long journey that is going to include some hiccups and obstacles as I set boundaries for her as a parent.

I am not perfect and I do not have a perfect method to build this relationship overnight, but I love her… and one day she will know that I love her.

It is about commitment and love – and this, we will provide. The changes we have already seen are remarkable. As we spend time with her and the boys, we will take things one day at a time. We are blessed to have this charming and bright young girl as our daughter, and are thankful for the chance to raise Madeline as our own.

PART 4

DESTINED: ADOPTEES AND BIRTH PARENT SHARE

14

Growing Up Adopted

Jerome Wong

"I have been brought up by awesome parents who are caring, loving and constantly sacrificing for me. They have taught me valuable life lessons, instilled discipline in me and given me strength in life."

Hi, I am Jerome, and I was adopted when I was just a day old. I first found out about my adoption when I was around six or seven years old. At that tender age, I did not really understand what adoption meant, nor did it strike me or affect my life in any way.

I had been brought up by awesome and loving parents who are caring, loving and constantly sacrificing for me. They have taught me valuable life lessons, instilled discipline in me and given me strength in life.

As I grew older, a part of me wanted to know who my biological parents were. Even though I am curious about who my birth parents are, I am really happy with my family. They are always there for me and I am so grateful that they took me in with loving hands.

Besides loving and caring for me, my mother introduced Jesus to me as well. When I was 10 years old, she urged me to join the Altar Servers at church. I made good friends there and understood the Mass better since the servers got to sit next to the priest during the Mass.

After I completed my PSLE (Primary School Leaving) examinations at 12 years old, I joined the wonderful church choir, Genesis II. I really enjoy the company of this crowd of awesome friends – they always bring a smile to my face. Singing in the choir also made me a stronger person, as it built my sense of confidence and helped me to make new friends while praising God.

Actually, I am not the only grandchild in our family who is adopted; a few of my first cousins were adopted too! With so much love from my parents, grandparents, godparents, uncles and aunts, my cousins and I know that even though we are all adopted, we have a wonderful family to watch our backs and love us as we grow and mature.

It is all right to be adopted. There is no shame in it; I can be who I want to be.

As for me, I love to dance and sing. I love the arts.

I know some parents would rather that their sons become an engineer or be a big buff guy, but my parents accept me and support my dreams of one day becoming a great dancer or a famous singer.

If you were adopted too, remember that you do not have to let anything hold you back. You do not need to feel different just because you were adopted.

You have the same chances like everyone else. Just because you were adopted does not mean that you are a stranger, an alien or an outcast. You are a person like everyone else. Remember, you are entitled to have dreams and aspirations just like everyone else.

Even if your parents question your dreams, do not be discouraged and do not use your adoption as an excuse or a means of escape.

Do not rebel or go against your parents. If you show that you are passionate about your interests, even the strictest parents may eventually be persuaded to let you pursue your dreams.

* Jerome is currently 16 years old. He was adopted from Mount Alvernia Hospital when he was just one day old.

15

I am Chang Hann

Chang Hann

"Being adopted makes me feel wanted, knowing that I was chosen. It is such a blessing and I will always be thankful to God and my parents."

I know who I am. I was adopted from an Indonesian family by my parents who are Chinese.

Sometimes I get asked why my complexion is so dark. Most of the time, we say it is because I do a lot of outdoor sports (which is true) as we do not always feel like sharing or think it is necessary to explain the whole adoption thing to others. I am not really bothered by it.

To me, being adopted makes me feel wanted, knowing that I was chosen. It is such a blessing and I will always be thankful to God and my parents.

Being adopted has not changed the way people think of me or the way I think of others. The community that I grew up in accepts me and does not judge me based on my adoption. This has strongly helped me to embrace the fact that I was adopted.

My family and friends have always been very supportive of what I do, and more importantly, who I am. This has helped me overcome thoughts of not being wanted and has helped me to accept it as a part of my identity.

A Family Who Sticks Together

My younger sister and I have always known about our adoption simply because my family has always been open and honest about it. I have pretty much known it all my life.

The fact that we are adopted has never been a problem for me or my sister. At this point in her life, she has not needed mentoring regarding adoption. I guess we are both secure about who we are – and that is a good thing.

To me, a family is a group of people who go through all aspects of life together, be it the good, the bad or the ugly – the works! Whether we share the same blood or not does not matter.

A family is one who sticks together. A family is always there for you. A family takes care of you and loves you like no one else does. A family stands with each other through thick or thin, come what may.

Two Sides Of A Story

I am currently not in touch with my birth family and do not know who they are. Since my adoption, I have been told I have met my birth mother once.

I used to think I would never search for my birth parents. But now, if I did find them, it would be to tell them I forgive them for everything. Because honestly, I feel my adoption has been nothing but a straight-up blessing.

To other adoptees, there are two things I want to say to you. The first is, there are always two sides to a story. It may seem like your birth parents left you because you were not good enough. Maybe it is true. Maybe it is not.

Maybe your birth parents could not afford to bring you up. Maybe they loved you so much they did not want you to grow up in an unhealthy environment.

There is a saying that goes, "If you love someone, set them free."

Your birth parents probably loved you. Do not hate them because they left you. First, find out why.

The second thing is, do not ever feel unwanted. Out of the 100 over children in the orphanage, your parents chose *you*. Your family loves *you*. God loves *you*. Your friends love *you*. Remember that.

To other adoptive parents, I would like to say that you have done a beautiful and courageous thing. Love your adopted children unconditionally so that they will always love themselves and believe in who they are.

My parents did that for me. I will always be thankful to them.

16

Letter To My Child

Birth Mother

"A moment in my arms, forever in my heart."
- Unknown

Dedicated to you, my baby:

I am your birth mommy. I am so sorry I had to place you for adoption. It hurts and pains me a lot, but I know you are having a better life right now. I miss you a lot.

I would rather let you grow up in a better environment than to let you suffer with me. I know saying sorry is not enough to mend your heart once you find out the truth and read this letter. Maybe when you are all grown up, you might realise and understand my reasons. I really hope you will not hate me for doing this and that you will forgive me.

Please do not ever think that I did not love you. I do love you a lot, but I am just incapable of being your mommy now and I really do not want you to suffer with me.

I want you to have a good and happy life. You must promise mommy you will grow up to be a good, healthy, smart and wonderful kid. And you must study hard too! I believe you can do anything!

Just remember that I will forever and always love you.

Sincerely,
Your Mommy

PART 5

ADOPTING
LATER IN LIFE

17

Being Older Parents

Yoke Fong

*"By choice, we have become a family, first in
our hearts, and finally in breath and being.
Great expectations are good; great experiences
are better."*

- Richard Fischer

My husband and I are proud parents of two adopted
daughters. At the time of their adoptions, Charis
was six years old in 2012 and Aletheia was three
in 2013.

We had married late in life because we were both busy with our
careers. Adoption was also a late consideration in our marriage.
Despite the fact that our combined age is more than 100 years
old, we are glad that "it is better late than never" because our
daughters have brought us so much joy.

Welcoming our two girls into our family has not been without
its challenges. However, these changes have stretched us yet
impacted us positively. We have learnt so much about ourselves
through them and intend for the joyful relationships to last a
lifetime.

Paperwork And Patience

We began the adoption process in 2004 whilst both of us were working in New Zealand. Paperwork and patience were two major hurdles we had to overcome. The adoption process was fraught with difficulties (and documentation!).

There is truth to the old adage; Awareness is half the battle won! The application process involved everything from gathering official statements about our financial status, mental and physical well-being, police reports and recommendations by referees, to taking compulsory courses on open adoption and completing several home visits.

Actually, that was the "easy" part of the application. The second part was waiting in vain for three years, with no child available to us for adoption. The average success rate of adoption in New Zealand was less than 30 percent per couple, so the likelihood of our finding a child was not very high.

Discouraged after all that time, we decided not to continue pursuing adoption in New Zealand and returned to Singapore at the end of 2008 where we repeated the whole adoption process – but this time, with a difference.

Doing It Differently

Firstly, we engaged the services of TOUCH Adoption Services (TAS), a branch of TOUCH Family Services. It proved to be the most crucial factor in our adoption application.

The experience and wise counsel of the TAS staff was key to the success of our adoption. When mental and physical fatigue set in, the social worker kept in close contact and encouraged us along the journey. She also introduced us many useful books and seminars.

Another big difference between trying to adopt in New Zealand versus Singapore is that we had more support and practical help from family and friends.

The officials from the Ministry of Social and Family Development (MSF) in Singapore were also very helpful in numerous ways. They quickly sought children who were suitable for us to adopt and arranged useful seminars for us to attend. Prior to the adoption, they were present at the weekly meetings we had with the girls and gave us detailed information about them.

After submitting our application to MSF through TOUCH Adoption Services in January 2009, we waited about eight months to receive news of Charis. Six months later in 2010, we were able to see her for the first time, followed by weekly visits.

Initial Challenges

Unfortunately, what should have been a happy time turned into a stressful period for everyone.

Charis became more fretful with each weekly visit she had with us. In fact, the visitations were stopped for several months because she was having nightmares. It seemed that she did not want us to be her adoptive parents. We had to demonstrate to MSF our determination and sincerity in wanting to adopt Charis, despite her becoming more withdrawn from us.

One important factor in our favour was that we would have more time to help Charis adjust to her new family as both my husband and I are semi-retired. We reminded MSF repeatedly of this, among other pertinent facts.

When we resumed the visits, Charis ran away as fast as she could whenever she saw us in the vicinity. We had to hide in order to watch her without upsetting her.

Eventually, one of the MSF officials managed to coax her out. We captured her attention with storytelling, origami, hula hula hoops, jewellery and photography. Our relatives also helped by inviting Charis to play with their children in their homes as well as swim in the pool and have fun at the playground.

The momentous day of our lives was when Charis came with us to watch a movie on 8 June 2011 – and stayed with us since then. I will never forget the movie we watched: *Kung Fu Panda*.

Having stayed in two foster homes, she was very insecure and was only introduced to us at about four years old. She needed daily hugs to be reassured that this is her "forever home" and we are her "forever daddy and mummy". These repeated assurances were vital towards helping her achieve emotional healing and stability.

Complete Overhaul

Our previous "quiet existence" vanished when the girls joined our family. Suddenly my husband and I became very busy – yet also fulfilled and happy! We had to rearrange our lives around the two girls starting with Charis in 2012, then Aletheia in 2013.

A year after we had adopted Charis, MSF informed us that Charis' birth father was willing to place his second daughter for adoption as well. We were the first choice for this consideration because Charis was happily settled and growing well in our home.

Naturally, we were surprised yet delighted because we thought Charis needed a playmate and companion to grow up with.

Aletheia was two years old at our first meeting. The first time we went out with her, she showed her strong disapproval of us by crying non-stop and vomited copiously in our car. It took many attempts at interacting with her before Aletheia finally accepted our visitation. When she met her birth sister, Charis encouraged her and played well with her.

After a year of paperwork, Aletheia finally joined our family when she was three years old. However, despite being younger and much smaller than her sister, she was more difficult to handle. She may have been light in weight, but she was certainly strong in will! This was obvious through her stubborn insistence on watching *Barney* on the TV at midnight or demanding to play with her toys whenever she wanted.

It was understandable why she was underweight; she ate poorly and had a poor appetite. Thankfully, our perseverance and hard work paid off. Three years on, her weight is now in the 50th percentile (from the previous third percentile). Like her sister, she too is a happy child!

Now Aletheia would ask us almost daily, "Do you love me?", especially when she is about to get disciplined for being naughty.

Loved As We Are

When we went out as a family, a common reaction we encountered was: "Your *grandchildren* are so cute and adorable!"

We are not perturbed by the misunderstandings and may occasionally correct the onlookers or simply smiled at the presumptuous thinking of some people.

Nor is our confidence shaken as older parents of young children because we know what we have committed to. We have made clear calculations about what is involved in bringing up the children and felt that we are adequately prepared to provide for them.

More importantly, our daughters accept us as we are, grey hair and all!

PART 6

DISCOVERIES

18

Pressure, I Need Pressure

Jane Samuel

"There are children playing in the streets who could solve some of my top problems in physics, because they have modes of sensory perception that I lost long ago."

- J. Robert Oppenheimer

We all have our ways of handling life's curve balls. Some catch them and deftly fling them right back. Some duck to the right or left to deflect them, are clipped only by the breeze as it flies on past, ruffling hairs but otherwise not stirring the deep soul.

Still others, our youngest daughter among them, take the full brunt of the ball square in the solar plexus, where the deep seat of her soul lies. Perhaps she will always remember deep down, at some cellular level, the many curve balls of her first life – her life before this life.

Abandonment.

Abject poverty mixed with neglect.

Adoption.

Universal shifts in her cosmic being.

To the naked eye, she continues on as before, though perhaps a bit more rigid in her body, nothing the untrained eye might pick up on. But I, mother to this sensory seeker, have learnt her language.

They say that communication is 20 percent verbal and 80 percent body language. It is the body language that speaks the loudest, reflecting the internal pleas that spell out danger and silent yelps that say:

"Hold me as close as I will let you – not as close as you think is needed – because I am feeling off-balance, afraid, not in control, out of my body."

Couch Sandwich

I remember the first time she spoke to me in this body lingo. We were doing something routine at home when things turned on end. I cannot recall what preceded it, but – as it often happened – my four-year-old was suddenly spinning out of control again.

Once again, I found myself searching in my new parental toolbox for some kernel of advice to rein her back in. I searched in the recesses of my mind for something I had read, or heard, or observed someone else do that I could pull out like a magic wand so that all would be quiet and normal again, and we would ride off into the sunset, she and I, like some awesome mother-daughter team.

Suddenly it came to me: How about the Couch Sandwich?

"Put her on the couch, pile the cushions on top and sit on her!" came the voice popping up out of some book or email from another parent, and into my head.

"Seriously," I argued with myself, "I could hurt her – she is only four!"

But the internal prompting to "Just do it!" simply would not go away.

So I plopped her on the couch, piled on the cushions and pressed gingerly on the lumpy mass, squatting, half my weight balanced above and half of it on top of her body buried underneath.

"More!" came her scream.

I released more weight.

"Harder!" she begged.

I released all my weight, thinking, "Surely I will snap her in half."

No crunching bones, no screams of pain, only the deep, now-regulated voice demanding, "Harder!"

Finding A Voice

That day I learnt something new: I learnt that she liked pressure. I learnt that she had a voice and could, if I guided her, learn to ask for what she needed.

Six years later now, she is much healed. Her soul deflects curve balls more regularly and she has learnt to slow her drive back to first gear or stop when needed; to keep her sensory seeking within appropriate boundaries most of the time.

However, when life transitions get to her – be it the school semester ending for the summer or her big sister leaving for college or vacation – *I know.*

Outside, she is appropriate and polite, almost exclusively, but her requests for "Pressure!" as she assumes a prone, stomach-down position on the nearest flat, soft surface tell me otherwise.

So I – or one of her sweet older sisters who also understands her needs – willingly climb on top of her to rein her back in. Show her she is safe. She is loved. She can regulate.

19

When Your Child Is Out Of Sync

Laurel Fanning

"There are no unwanted children, just unfound families."

- National Adoption Center, USA

I still recall those days in 2004 when we sat in our adoption coordinator's conference in the United States, getting our training in anticipation of the arrival of our daughter. We were about to adopt Elena, at two years old, from the baby home in Vidnoe, Moscow Region, Russia.

Having just gotten married three weeks prior, my husband and I had put in our application for adoption in September 2004. We had already decided we were ready and wanted to get going. After all, we were not getting any younger!

Having no other children, we spent hours reading all the books on adoption and scouring the pages of *Adoptive Families* magazine month after month.

Some of the subject matter was very reassuring. Some of it terrified us.

Getting Our Baby

When we finally got "the call" in March 2005, we hurriedly made the arrangements for what would be the first of two trips to Moscow.

Russia did a blind referral process; in other words, they had selected a child for us. We did not even know what she looked like.

All we knew was her name and that she had had a close call with a potentially bad medical condition. However, we were assured that all was now well.

When we arrived in Moscow, our adoption coordinator explained to us the details about the circumstances regarding Elena's birth. It turns out that our daughter had been put up for adoption at birth. However, she had been housed in a hospital with what the coordinator described as "poor care" for the first six months of her life, before getting placed in the baby home until her adoption.

Early Life Impact

We did not know it at the time, but those first six months created challenges that would stay with her, in some way, for the rest of her life.

We quickly realised that we did not know everything we needed to know. Somehow, all the studying we had done and the training that we had received about adoption seemed inadequate. The rubber was now hitting the road!

Not having had children before, we were always wondering, "Is this a developmental problem?", "Is it an adoption thing?" or "Is this a typical two-year-old thing?"

We knew there were issues as certain behaviours of hers that started to manifest, but we did not know what was causing them nor did we know what to do about it.

There were disastrous play dates, sleepovers, meetings with new relatives and other people she did not know. We observed that when she could not be in total control of the situation around her, she would "lose it".

We later learned at a seminar that when babies are not nurtured and left to themselves (such as while in the hospital), the portion of their brain called the amygdala will actually wire differently to focus on the "fight or flight" reaction. They try to teach themselves how to manage their environment as much as possible in their attempt to take care of their own needs.

Discovering The Root

Throughout Elena's years at preschool, kindergarten and up through second grade (eight years old), we had intermittent interfaces with occupational therapists. However, nothing seemed to be working. Either we did not quite understand or they did not explain well enough for us to understand the root causes and the appropriate mitigation for the issues we were having.

In the summer of 2011, we moved from the United States to Singapore, for what was to be an indeterminate assignment with a new employer. We totally underestimated the effect the transition would have on her. It further amplified all the control issues she was already dealing with.

She struggled in school, seemingly forgetting much of what she had learnt in school the year before. We started to panic when, almost halfway through the school year, she was doing worse academically instead of better.

Fortunately, a therapist led us to a local firm that conducted cognitive assessment and other related services. Through the assessment they did with our daughter, they found a few areas of cognitive trouble, including her ability to commit things to long-term memory.

Overall, however, they said the biggest thing that was likely getting in the way of her academic learning was *sensory processing issues*.

Finally, we had a name for the reason behind some of the behaviours that had been plaguing her since she was born!

Understanding The Problem

We were referred to an occupational therapist to do a formal sensory assessment of her. In the process, we read *The Out-of-Sync Child – Recognizing and Coping with Sensory Processing Disorder** by Carol Kranowitz, which helped us immensely.

It provided a good explanation of all the base sensory systems that may be affected, including the tactile, vestibular (balance), proprioceptive (muscles, joints and internal organs), visual and auditory systems. It also showed parents what to look for, comparing "normal" behaviours to "abnormal" behaviours based on sensory issues and how these problems can be dealt with.

We were particularly struck by the section on page 37, which outlined 13 possible causes of sensory processing disorder (SPD). Our daughter had nine of the 13 primary reasons why kids typically get SPD!

From what we gleaned, her base systems had never fully developed, as her brain had totally focused on survival issues. Because of this, she was constantly operating at a high level of arousal, trying to manage all the input from her environment at once.

With a good dose of occupational therapy, alongside a programme of therapeutic horse-riding, her sensory development has really improved today.

Now, at 11 years old, she is doing very well, but she will always struggle with some of her base issues. The biggest problem we have now is dealing with a "tween"!

While she struggles with being as mature and independent as possible, she is also a very loving and caring child who will share anything she has with you.

A Word For Parents

For adoptive parents, especially those who adopt from institutions, our word of advice to you is this: Make sure you do your homework.

Learn what to look for if you suspect issues and be ready to get help for your child as soon as possible. Do not be afraid of it. Face it head-on and realise that by getting them help early on, you will be giving them one of the best gifts you could ever give as a parent.

We discovered that the road was not paved. We have had some bumps. But we have learnt a lot and we just keep going. We have a wonderful daughter. We are still a family!

---

* *Kranowitz, Carol,* Introduction to The Out-Of-Sync Child: Recognizing and Coping With Sensory Processing Disorder, *revised edition, Perigee, 2005*

PART 7

WHY NOT FOSTER

20

A Fostering Journey

Lynette Chiu

"It is hard to see a cherished child leave, but we are always thankful for the opportunity to have loved them."

Ray and I have always wanted to help children.

In the early 1990s, before we were married, we used to volunteer at Club Rainbow, an organisation whose aim is to bring cheer to seriously or terminally ill children. We volunteered as befrienders at camps or helped to do balloon sculpting at tea events.

We enjoyed contributing to these ad-hoc sessions, but we wanted to do more. After we got married, I tutored at a Children's Home. I went twice a week to teach the kids. On weekends, Ray and I took them for outings.

The time at the Children's Home was an eye-opener as I did not realise that there were so many children in need of care. It was very fulfilling and allowed us to volunteer on a regular basis.

Yet, once again, Ray and I felt we wanted to do more than that.

In 2004, we made a decision to open up our homes and provide a safe and nurturing environment to children who had been abused, neglected or abandoned. When our son was a year old, we took in our first foster child.

We had started providing foster care on our own, but in 2006, we officially came under the umbrella of Ministry of Social and Family Development (MSF).

Eleven years on, we are currently looking after our fifth foster child.

Because We Can

People ask how we do it, and the answer is, we just do.

We treat each child who comes into our home as ours. We love them, we teach them, we entertain them, we keep them safe and healthy – and when it is time for them to go, we say goodbye.

It is hard to see a cherished child leave, but we are always thankful for the opportunity to have loved them.

People ask why we do it, and the answer is, because we can.

We have an extra room in our home for any child who needs a safe place. We live simply so we have time and energy and resources to foster children.

We do this because we believe that when we bring a child into our home, we are opening their eyes to another way of living.

These children are often taken from trying circumstances. Unless they are shown a different lifestyle, they may grow up mirroring the difficult lives that they see around them.

Changing Lives

The decision to become a foster a parent has been a life-changing one. Before we embarked on this journey, there were countless questions and doubts running through our minds:

Would we be able to do this?

Would we be able to love the children we foster as our own?

What happens when they leave?

Would we be able to take the loss?

How would our own children deal with sharing their parents, their home, their toys?

Would our extended family want these children in their lives?

Would the foster children's biological parents impact our lives in any way?

However, in the end, while those questions were valid and important, we realised it was impossible to answer all of them. The only question that needed to be asked was of ourselves: Were *we* ready to commit to a child and see him/her through a difficult time of his/her life?

With every child we fostered, the questions that came with them changed. Each child came with different circumstances and challenges that we could neither predict nor control.

However, through commitment to the children, we were able to walk with them as they went through a time of their life where all they really needed was someone to be by their side.

Like anything worth doing, fostering has had its share of sacrifices and compromises, but it has been one of the most enriching and meaningful experiences of our lives. We have never regretted the decision to become foster parents.

People ask how long we want to carry on doing it, and the answer is, as long as we are able to.

There are still many children who need secure and stable environments to grow up in. One day, we hope to have more than one extra room to care for these children. We still want to do more.

For more information on fostering in Singapore, call MSF at +65 63548799 or email fostering@msf.gov.sg

PART 8

FROM THE PROFESSIONALS

21

Merging Hearts With Hope And Love

Wong Wei Lei
Senior Social Worker and Adoptive Mother
TOUCH Family Services

Heartbroken, resolute but emotions torn;
Inconsolable... a deep and painful loss she does mourn.
"Will my child hate me when he is grown?"
"Not so, when gently and early, the seeds of truth are sown..."
"He will learn that, bravely and painfully,
with him you did part.
But forever and with love, he will remain in your heart."

Her shame and guilt so overwhelmingly felt.
Affirming her strength and courage little did help.
As I watched the birth mother say goodbye to her child,
I pray God's comfort for her as she walks the next mile.
Uncertainty and awkwardness was felt for a while,
As adoptive parents and birth mother met,
all talk came to a lull.

Intense emotions were felt as tears welled.
All eyes fixed on child, every heart, with love, swelled.
"So grateful to you for blessing us with a precious baby.
We will love him as our very own and divine destiny."
"Thank you for being my child's loving family…"
A reply spoken not in words but through
tears that flowed freely.

A meeting that started with apprehension and uncertainty
Became a merging of hearts with greater
assurance and empathy.
A poignant moment that will stay vivid in their memory
And affirm their child when he hears
this as part of his adoption story.
With all the mixed emotions,
the moment was not prolonged.
Placing the child in new parents' arms,
birth mother struggled to move on.

Holding her shoulders, I knew no words
could comfort her heart.
Meeting her child's adoptive parents had,
hopefully, helped her to part.
Their warmth and kind words had
affirmed her courageous plan
And assured her that her child is in good hands.
I reminded her, "You did not abandon
your child or give him away.
Rather, you chose a loving family
who will walk with him all the way."

With wet eyes and beaming smiles,
adoptive parents stood in awe
As they beheld baby dressed in new romper, mittens and all.
They exclaimed, "This is surreal!"
with hearts full and joy exuberant.
Their lives touched by this miracle of life is no mere accident.
As they rejoice in every milestone and journey with their son,
He will know how deeply he is loved as their treasured one.

A colleague once said that it is like
going through a sliding door
With strong emotions that lie so low in
one room while in the other soar.
In one, I hold the hand of a mother
who has to painfully let go.
In the other, I celebrate with parents with
a long-awaited child to hold.
While I listen to one who has to hide her pain;
her story to others untold,
I share the joy of elated parents as their new journey unfolds.

I pray the pain does lessen, knowing joy
has replaced the parents' tears,
With hope that the child will understand in his grown years,
When told by parents that his first mother
is someone he can hold dear;
That he is loved by two families and no less,
compared to all his peers.
My hope is that love, openness and empathy will replace fear.
Then healing will touch all who suffered
such loss, far and near.

22

Poignant Reflections

Teo Seok Bee

*"We can find consolation that one child adopted
is one life changed and a family transformed."*

Teo Seok Bee is the Senior Manager of TOUCH Family Services. In 2001, she helped to set up TOUCH Adoption Services after a study trip to the United States of America with the then Ministry of Community Youth and Sports.

In this collection of short vignettes, she recounts some of the encounters and exchanges she has been privileged to witness over the past 14 years as an adoption worker.

* * * * * *

The Longing

The year was 2002. The venue was an orphanage that would take a bumpy four-hour ride from Phnom Penh, Cambodia.

The scene was an unforgettable one as our van backed slowly out of the driveway of the orphanage when it was time to leave. The 14-year-old girl ran after our van, shouting:

"Take me to Singapore. I want to be your sister!"

It was a heart-wrenching moment. This girl had seen numerous visitors and adoptive parents walk through their doors, sometimes leaving with a younger child in tow as a new member of their families.

Knowing that Cambodia has a rule that limits adoption to only children aged eight and below, this girl made a plea of a different kind – probably not the first – for a family outside of the institution she had lived for the past 14 years.

After all these years since that day, the scene has remained vivid in my memory. I sometimes wonder how she or her peers is/are doing today. She would be in her late 20s now, probably forced to leave the institution and fend for herself in the harsh world outside.

Is she married? What emotional scars have been left in her young mind? What intervention could have happened to help her make sense of her difficult background?

For the many children who get adopted, there are countless others who would never know what it means to belong to a family they can call their own. Whilst it would take many years to fully address this, for now, we can find consolation that one child adopted is one life changed and a family transformed.

* * * * * *

The First Date

As the name was called out, a nanny walked into the room with a child in her arms. Mr and Mrs Tan got up quickly from their chairs, their eyes fixed on the child – the precious one they had been waiting for what seemed like years.

Mrs Tan could not hide her pent-up emotions any longer and tears flowed down her cheeks as she gently took the child from the nanny's arms.

Together with a colleague, we had accompanied eight families on the inaugural trip to Chongqing, China, in 2005, to meet their adopted children for the first time and to finalise the adoption proceedings.

It boasted a first in many areas – this was the first batch of adoptive parents being welcomed in China since the signing of the bilateral adoption agreement between Singapore and China.

For some of the families, it was their first visit to China. Naturally, it was the first time they all met their children…

The 10-day visit was a defining moment for those eight families. From the formal interview and signing procedures to the informal sightseeing tours, joy of the highest kind mixed with baby cries filled the air.

Whilst we were impressed with the attention to detail in arranging for baby strollers, cots and baby tubs in the hotel rooms, we were elated with the progress some of the children made in just 10 days of individual care and attention given.

It was an honour and privilege to share such significant moments with the families. We saw our vision played out during the trip – the fulfillment of a dream – of couples wanting to parent a child and a child finding a permanent loving family.

* * * * * *

The Dilemma

"My mum wants me to abort the child. We are in the hospital now."

The desperate plea for help came through a text message. I had met J and her boyfriend –both in their 20s – a month earlier to talk about their plans to place their unborn child for adoption. J's mother had found out about her pregnancy and insisted on an abortion.

After much persuasion and pleading, her parents agreed to sit down and discuss the matter with their daughter. J's mother was highly emotional and distraught. It soon came to my attention that the family was grappling with more issues than just their daughter's pregnancy – there were financial issues and health issues as well as another child who had left the house.

Despite the daughter's pleas, J's mother was insistent about the abortion. Her father was ambivalent. The hospital gave a cooling-off period over the weekend before scheduling the procedure for Monday.

The weekend saw a frantic power play between all parties trying to sway each other's minds. It soon became clear what the decision would be.

I visited J on Monday at the hospital after her third injection of prostaglandin to induce labour contractions. She had come to terms with going along with her mother's decision.

"That is how we can remain as a family and I will have peace," she explained.

Silence filled the air. There was really nothing more I could say or offer except to hold her hands as I sat by her.

When faced with the dilemma of abortion or adoption, many birth families go through pains weighing the pros and cons of each decision against the values they hold strong.

To J's mother, abortion was an easier way out. Her daughter would not have to live with the shame of being ridiculed by neighbours and relatives when they see her bulging tummy. She would not have to go through the pains of delivering the baby, only to hand him/her to some strangers who may or may not treat their child well. The child would not grow up feeling he/she was unwanted by his/her birth family.

To J and her father, it was the way to maintain peace and harmony in the family.

Was it really an easier decision? Unknown to her mother, J had had a previous abortion and it had haunted her for the past two years. But she could not tell her mom that she knew what it was like to have an abortion – and now, to have to do it twice.

She could not tell her mom she regretted it. Her mom would not be able to take another blow.

* * * * * *

The Choice

"We do not want to shop for a child. We will let you decide."

I was taken aback by these words from a prospective couple who was offered the possibility of two potential matches of babies placed for adoption. This couple had no preference as to ethnicity, gender or age of the child they wanted to adopt. They were also open to a child with special needs.

I was incredulous as I thought to myself, "Are you sure you want me to make such a major decision on your behalf?"

I have met many couples who made very specific requests of their preferences and who would even ask for more information about the background of the birth parents – but this was the first time a couple entrusted me with such a heavy responsibility, with no questions asked!

I have always posed this challenge to prospective adopters: Look not a child for the family, but a family for the child. This couple took up the challenge literally!

Some of you may wonder – so did I make the choice for them? The answer is, *certainly not!*

In the end, the couple chose the match with an earlier EDD (expected date of delivery). The choice proved to be right, for the second birth family subsequently decided to raise the child themselves!

* * * * *

The Reunion

The reunion was initiated by the adoptive parents. "Can I really meet them?" The birth mother could not believe she would ever see the child she had borne six years ago.

On the day of the reunion, the adoptive parents were early. Their son was shy. Needing support, the birth mother subsequently arrived with her sister and friend.

The adoptive parents updated the birth mother of the child's progress, his likes and dislikes, and how the family had been doing all these years. The birth mother shared that she had completed her studies and had started working.

The short meeting went on smoothly, with everyone sensitive and conscious of each other. The presence of the child diffused all awkwardness as the birth family tried to engage a conversation with him.

The birth mother was assured that the child was loved and well taken care of. After waving her goodbye, it was not until after the adoptive family was out of sight that the birth mother burst into tears, much to everyone's surprise. Her composure earlier had given no outward sign of the emotions that were going on inside.

Seeing how her child has developed, how his adoptive parents have given him the unconditional love and how they had initiated the reunion, she was filled with gratitude and joy, affirmed that she had made the right decision six years ago.

She continued her gaze in the direction of the departing family, heartened that she was given a chance to show her love to the child, even if it was from a distance.

PART 9

WHAT YOU NEED TO KNOW ABOUT ADOPTION

What You Need To Know About Adoption

Before embarking on the child adoption journey, it is important that prospective adoptive parents familiarise themselves with the steps and requirements involved in the adoption process. It is also good for them to know what to do and what not to do when they begin raising their adopted child. This will help them to consider and adequately plan for the essential resources and time needed, and prepare them emotionally and psychologically to raise their child. The information, recommendation and references contained in this section serve as an easy guide to help adoptive parents in their adoption journey.

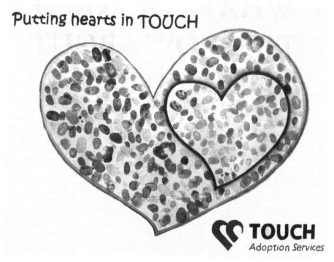

A masterpiece painted by nearly a hundred individuals touched by adoption at TOUCH Adoption Services' Annual Party in 2014.

Frequently Asked Questions About Child Adoption

1. How do I go about adopting a child?

Step 1 – Self Evaluation and Research

You should evaluate your motivation and readiness to adopt, discuss it with significant people in your life, read books on adoption or talk to adoptive parents.

In Singapore, it is a requirement that you attend a Pre-Adoption Briefing/Talk.

Step 2 – Home Study

You should get a Home Study Report (HSR) done by accredited agencies prior to identifying a foreign child for adoption. A HSR is an assessment of a prospective adopter's suitability and readiness to adopt a child.

For a list of updated accredited agencies in Singapore approved by the Ministry of Social and Family Development to conduct Home Study Reports, please go to: http://app.msf.gov.sg/Adoption/Apply-for-Home-Study-Report.

Step 3 – Sourcing For A Child

Prospective adopters may source for a child locally or overseas. The documentation, costs, length of time, procedures, approval processes and child-matching criteria differs for each country and agency.

Step 4 – Legalisation and Citizenship

You will have to apply for a dependant's pass for the child's entry into Singapore for the adoption process, if the child is not a Singaporean. The application form is available on the Ministry of Social and Family Development's website (*http:// app.msf.gov.sg/Adoption*).

You will also need to engage a lawyer who can facilitate the legalisation of the adoption in Singapore or your home country. After the adoption order is obtained, you may apply for citizenship for your child.

2. Am I eligible to adopt?

General Requirements

Prospective adopters should love children, and hold positive views towards adoption and parenting. They should be healthy, have a stable marriage and be of sound financial status.

Prospective adopters should be residents of Singapore.

Age

You and your spouse must be at least 25 years old and at least 21 years older than the child to be adopted.

Maximum age gap between adopter and child

Both you and your spouse should not be more than 50 years older than the child.

Foreign prospective adopters (including permanent residents in Singapore) should consult their respective embassies as to their eligibility to adopt while residing in Singapore.

3.   How long is the adoption process?

The length of time differs greatly for each country and agency. Do check with the respective agencies and authorities in your country.

In Singapore, the Home Study Report process takes about five to twelve weeks, depending on which agency you have chosen to work with. The waiting time to obtain a dependant's pass is about two weeks. The legal process takes about three to six months. Each Home Study Report is valid for two years in Singapore.

4.   How can I be sure that my adopted child will bond with me?

Bonding is a journey, not an arrival. You can build attachment with your child by responding to your child's cry promptly, coaxing your child to make frequent eye contact and maintaining physical contact with your child as much as possible during the initial months. It is important to minimise your child's time with other caregivers by jealously guarding your time spent with him/her.

Establish a routine and enjoy giving your child a soothing massage and rocking your child to sleep in your arms to keep your child feeling calm and regulated.

Since feeding, bathing, changing of diapers, carrying and soothing are associated with feelings of comfort and safety, parents should attend to these tasks in order to help their child build trust and feel secure with them rather than with another caregiver.

Building a strong attachment during the initial months/year will help parents be more attuned to their child's needs and feel emotionally more in sync with their child.

5.   Should I tell my child he/she was adopted? When and how should I do it?

Transparency builds trust and intimacy. We recommend that you, as adoptive parents, be open and transparent with your adopted child about his/her birth history. You are encouraged to do so as early as possible with age-appropriate explanations.

Disclosure is an ongoing process. Practise when the child is young by introducing the idea of adoption through reading children's books about adoption or using daily events and media programmes. Present sensitive information in a calm and matter-of-fact way. Validate and process with your child his/her feelings, questions and wishes.

Adoption Disclosure talks are available several times annually to assist you in your understanding and preparation. Check for workshop dates at: *https://app.adoption.gov.sg/RegisterWorkshopIntro.aspx*

Joining and being part of a support group could also help your child see that there are other adoptive families like yours.

Adoptive parenting has its unique issues and a support group could be a safe place for sharing and discussions.

6.   What if my child's biological parents want to take him/ her back when he/she is older?

Once the adoption is legalised, biological parents have permanently and irreversibly relinquished their rights over the child. You will be considered the legal parents of the child. Thereafter, it is against the law for the biological parents to make any demands or exert any right over the child.

Positive Adoption Language

The words we use say a lot about how we really think and feel. Words can either hurt or heal. The conscious and consistent use of positive adoption language conveys our values and affirms birth parents, adopted children and adoptive parents in the conviction that adoption is a valid way to build a family. Therefore, it is important to use terms that are respectful and non-judgmental.

Positive Language	Negative Language
Biological / Birth parent	*Natural / Real parent*
Tummy mummy / Daddy	*Real / Own mommy / Daddy*
Birth child	*Own / Real child*
My child	*My adopted child*
Born to unmarried parents	*Illegitimate child*
Placed for adoption / Make an adoption plan / Found you a loving family	*Give up / Give away / Surrender*
Search	*Track down parents*
To parent a child	*To keep a child*
He / She was adopted	*He / She is adopted*

What NOT To Say To An Adoptive Parent or Adopted Child & Creative Ways To Answer These Insensitive Questions

Adoptive families are not as common and sometimes, people's comments and questions come across as hurtful and insensitive.

Oftentimes, they do not stem from malice but rather, from ignorance, preconceived ideas, unprocessed understanding and discomfort with the subject.

When faced with such questions, we can choose to ***W.I.S.E. Up**:

W	*Walk away or do not respond.*
I	*Say, "It is private, so I would rather not discuss it." Or change the subject.*
S	*Share something about your adoption story.*
E	*Educate others about adoption.*

**Schoettle, Marilyn, W.I.S.E. UpPowerbook, Center for Adoption Support and Education, 2000*

For Children:

Even after you talk to your child about adoption, it will not be surprising when his friends and peers ask questions that you may find sensitive, intrusive and even rude.

As parents, you can equip him/her with answers so that your child will feel empowered to handle them confidently.

Here are some of the frequently asked questions and ready answers for your child to learn:

1. *Is that your real mom (or dad)?*
   "Why are you asking?"
   "Would I call her mom if she wasn't?"
   "Yes, a real mom is the person who takes care of you."

2. *Why didn't your real mom keep you?*
   "She couldn't take care of me, but my mom will always take care of me."
   "This is stuff we talk about at home."
   "It is personal; I don't feel like answering that question."

3. *Where are you from?*
   "What do you mean? Do you want to know my ethnicity or where I was born?"
   "I was born in Indonesia, but I am now a Singaporean, like you."
   "I'm from another planet."

For Adults:

1. *How much did you pay for him/her? Wow, it's so expensive!*
   "Oh, he/she is priceless! How much did she pay when you gave birth to your child?"

2. *Why did his / her birth parents give him / her away?*
    "Well, we feel it must have been a difficult decision for his / her birth parents but they did what they felt was best for him / her at that point of their lives."

3. *Your child does not look like you (father) at all!*
    "Oh, I think she takes after her mother."

4. *How come your children look so different, one white, one brown?*
    "(Answer with a smile...) One is born in the day and the other at night!"

5. *Why don't you adopt someone of the same race?*
    "He/She is meant for us."

6. *How lucky you are or lucky he/she is!*
    "Actually, we are the lucky ones to have him/her!"

7. *You are such nice people to take him/her.*
    "Oh, and you are nice to have your children too."

8. *Why can't you have your own children?*
    "He / She IS my own child. Did you mean biological child?"

9. *Now that you have adopted, God will bless you with your own child very soon.*
    "Thanks, God has indeed blessed me with more than I have asked for."

10. *What if his/her birth parents want him/her back?*
    "We have gone through several levels of checks and legalisation to make sure all parties are sure of this adoption."

11. *Where did he/she come from?*
    "Do you mean which country he/she is from? Oh, it is [name of country]."

12. *Did you breastfeed your child?*
    "I wish I did. It does wonders. Did you?"

13. *Why would you want to parent someone else's child?*
    "He is my son and I am his forever daddy."

14. *Why do you want to tell your child you are not her real parents?*
    "We are her real and forever parents, and we tell our child about her biological parents because we love her and it is not something to be ashamed of."

15. *Are you his coach/teacher/helper?*
    "I am everything to him."

16. *Person gives a triangular stare from daddy to mummy to baby, then says "Is this child..."*
    "Complete the answer for him, *"She is a lovely baby, isn't she?"*"

Recommended Books On Adoption For Children

1. **A Mother For Choco**
   Author: Keiko Kasza
   Publisher: Puffin Books
   ISBN-10: 0-399-24191-4
   ISBN-13: 978-0-399-24191-8

2. **Tell Me Again About The Night I Was Born**
   Author: Jamie Lee Curtis
   Publisher: HarperCollins
   ISBN-10: 0-06-4-43581-4
   ISBN-13: 978-0-06-443581-9

3. **A Blessing From Above**
   Author: Patti Henderson
   Publisher: Golden Books
   ISBN-10: 0-375-82866-4
   ISBN-13: 978-0-375-82866-9

4. **God Found Us You**
   Author: Lisa Tawn Bergren
   Publisher: HarperCollins
   ISBN-10: 0-06-113176-8
   ISBN-13: 978-0-06-113176-9

5. **How I Was Adopted**
   Author: Joanna Cole
   Publisher: HarperCollins
   ISBN-10: 0-688-17055-2
   ISBN-13: 978-0-688-17055-4

6.   **We Just Want You To Know**
     Author/Publisher: Andrea Yee
     ISBN: 978-981-08-2214-9

7.   **Why Am I Blue?**
     Author: Melanie Lee
     Publisher: MPH Publishing
     ISBN-10: 967-415-206-7
     ISBN-13: 978-967-415-206-2

8.   **The Day We Met You**
     Author: Phoebe Koehler
     Publisher: Aladdin Paperbacks
     ISBN-10: 0-689-80964-6
     ISBN-13: 978-0-689-80964-4

Recommended Books On Adoption For Parents

1   **Our Very Own – Stories Celebrating Adoptive Families**
     Publisher: TOUCH Family Services Limited
     ISBN: 978-981-08-6940-3

2   **Holding Time**
     Author: Martha G Welch
     Publisher: Simon & Schuster
     ISBN-10: 0671-68878-2
     ISBN-13: 978-0-671-68878-3

3   **Raising Adopted Children**
    Author: Lois Ruskai Melina
    Publisher: William Morrow Paperbacks
    ISBN-10: 0-06-095717-4
    ISBN-13: 978-0-06-095717-9

4   **Twenty Things Adopted Kids Wish Their Adoptive Parents Knew**
    Author: Sherrie Eldridge
    Publisher: Delta
    ISBN: 978-0-440-50838-0

5   **The Connected Child: Bring Hope And Healing To Your Adoptive Family**
    Author: Karyn B. Purvis
    Publisher: McGraw-Hill Education
    ISBN-10: 0-07-147500-1
    ISBN-13: 978-0-07-147500-6

6   **The Primal Wound: Understanding The Adopted Child**
    Author: Nancy Newton Verrier
    Publisher: Gateway Press
    ISBN-10: 0-9636480-0-4
    ISBN-13: 978-0-9636480-0-6

7   **Parenting The Hurt Child: Helping Adoptive Families Heal And Grow**
    Author: Gregory Keck and Regina Kupecky
    Publisher: NavPress
    ISBN-10: 1-57683-314-3
    ISBN-13: 978-1-57683-314-8

8 **Attaching In Adoption: Practical Tools For Today's Parents**
Author: <u>Deborah D. Gray</u>
Publisher: Jessica Kingsley Pub
ISBN-10: 0-944934-29-3
ISBN-13: 978-0-944934-29-6

9 **The Family Of Adoption**
Author: Dr Joyce <u>Maguire Pavao</u>
Publisher: Beacon Press; Reprint edition (February 20, 2005)
ISBN-10: 0-8070-2827-4
ISBN-13: 978-0-8070-2827-8

10 **Creating Loving Attachments: Parenting with PACE to Nurture Confidence and Security in the Troubled Child**
Author: Kim S. Golding
Publisher: Jessica Kingsley Publishers Ltd
ISBN: 978-1-84905-227-6

11 **Parenting With Love And Logic**
Author: Foster Cline and Jim Fay
Publisher: Pinon Press
ISBN-10: 1-57683-954-6
ISBN-13: 978-1-5-683-954-6

REFERENCES

Verrier, Nancy, (2003), "The Primal Wound: Understanding the Adopted Child", Verrier Publishing, 2003

Kranowitz, Carol, Introduction to The Out-Of-Sync Child: Recognizing and Coping With Sensory Processing Disorder, revised edition, Perigee, 2005

Schoettle, Marilyn, W.I.S.E. Up Powerbook, Center for Adoption Support and Education, 2000

Scripture quotations marked NIV are taken from the Holy Bible, New International Version®. NIV®. Copyright ©1973, 1978, 1984 by International Bible Society. Used by permission of Zondervan. All rights reserved [Biblica]

About Touch Community Services

Who We Are

TOUCH Community Services (TOUCH) is a not-for-profit charitable organisation. We were officially registered in 1992 and have been a member of the National Council of Social Service since 1994.

How We Started

The work of TOUCH started in 1986 as a service for latch-key children in the neighbourhoods of Clementi and Jurong.

It has become a multi-service organisation today, with an integrated network of 17 services, 15 centres and 21 children's clubs located at different parts of Singapore.

Who We Serve

Over the last 23 years, TOUCH has reached out to many individuals from all religions and races, including children, youth, families, people with special needs and healthcare needs as well as the elderly.

To promote greater awareness and exposure to overseas community work, we also partner closely with organisations in various countries in the areas of community development and humanitarian relief.

ABOUT TOUCH ADOPTION SERVICES

TOUCH Adoption Services is a service of TOUCH Family Services, which is affiliated to TOUCH Community Services.

Our Mission

At TOUCH Adoption Services, we believe that every child is a precious gift and deserves a permanent and loving family. We seek to be a bridge helping every parent fulfil the dream of loving and caring for a child through adoption. We help prospective adopters in their adoption process, as well as prepare them for their role as adoptive parents.

Our Focus

We service the children, the adoptive community and birth families. We endeavour to:

- Advocate & Empower
- Educate & Equip
- Facilitate & Place

Our Services

- Home study and post placement reports
- Talks and workshops for prospective adopters and adoptive parents
- Child placement
- Counselling for birth parents, adoptees, prospective adopters and adoptive parents

- Support group for the adoptive community – TAFNET – TOUCH Adoptive Families Network
- Loan and sale of adoption related resources

Artist James Leong was inspired by our gathering of adoptive families at Botanic Gardens in August 2015.

Our Contact

Address: 5 Stadium Walk
                Leisure Park Kallang
                #04-05/06
                Singapore 397693

Tel: +65 6709 8400
Fax: +65 6709 8416
Email: adoption@touch.org.sg
Website: *http://adoption.tcs.org.sg*
                http://www.touch.org.sg